More Praise for *The Heart of Leadership*

"*The Heart of Leadership* addresses the primary stumbling block for leaders—themselves! If you want to improve how you lead others, you must first improve how you lead yourself. This great little book shows you how."

—**Daniel S. Harkavy, CEO, author, and Executive Coach, Building Champions, Inc.**

"*The Heart of Leadership* extends and deepens the bestselling leadership models pioneered by Mark Miller. This book is clear, compelling, and of real practical value. Keep it on hand—a small investment of time will yield a lifetime of dividends, in your life as well as in your career."

—**Jeff Rosensweig, Associate Professor of International Business and Finance and Director, Global Perspectives Program, Goizueta Business School, Emory University**

"There's a difference between potential leaders with raw talent and great leaders with real influence. Mark's book reveals the foundational difference—it's all about leadership character."

—**Tony Morgan, author and Chief Strategic Officer and founder of TonyMorganLive.com**

"Mark Miller's *The Heart of Leadership* immediately creates a place for personal discovery. As I read each page, I was no longer thinking of Blake, the main character, but myself. Blake's journey of discovery became my own. This is about the 'life' of leadership and how it reaches within and without, having profound and long-lasting impact. It's about being unselfishly driven and highly motivated. It is about how others within the workplace and within our lives benefit from our personal resolve to lead from the perspective that others matter."

—**Clifton L. Taulbert, author of *Eight Habits of the Heart* and President, The Freemount Corporation/Building Community Institute**

"There are so many buzzwords in business that claim to be the answer to all leadership woes. The truth is that leadership is all about the people, and to have success with people, read *The Heart of Leadership*, and watch your leadership soar to a whole new level."

—**Todd Nielsen, author and COO, JMARK Business Solutions**

The Heart of Leadership

OTHER BOOKS BY MARK MILLER

The Secret of Teams
The Secret of Teams Field Guide

With Ken Blanchard

Great Leaders Grow
The Secret

The Heart of Leadership

Becoming a Leader People Want to Follow

Mark Miller

Berrett–Koehler Publishers, Inc.

a BK Business book

Berrett-Koehler Publishers, Inc.
1333 Broadway, Suite 1000
Oakland, CA 94612-1921
Tel: (510) 817-2277   Fax: (510) 817-2278   www.bkconnection.com

Ordering Information

Quantity sales. Special discounts are available on quantity purchases by corporations, associations, and others. For details, contact the "Special Sales Department" at the Berrett-Koehler address above.

Individual sales. Berrett-Koehler publications are available through most bookstores. They can also be ordered directly from Berrett-Koehler:
Tel: (800) 929-2929; Fax: (802) 864-7626; www.bkconnection.com

Orders for college textbook/course adoption use. Please contact Berrett-Koehler: Tel: (800) 929-2929; Fax: (802) 864-7626.

Distributed to the US trade and internationally by Penguin Random House Publisher Services.

Production Management: Michael Bass Associates
Cover Design: Irene Morris

Berrett-Koehler and the BK logo are registered trademarks of Berrett-Koehler Publishers, Inc.

Printed in the United States of America

Berrett-Koehler books are printed on long-lasting acid-free paper. When it is available, we choose paper that has been manufactured by environmentally responsible processes. These may include using trees grown in sustainable forests, incorporating recycled paper, minimizing chlorine in bleaching, or recycling the energy produced at the paper mill.

Library of Congress Cataloging-in-Publication Data

Miller, Mark.
    The heart of leadership : becoming a leader people want to follow / Mark Miller.—First Edition.
        pages cm
    ISBN 978-1-60994-960-0 (hardcover)
    1. Leadership. I. Title.
HD57.7.M5375 2013
658.4'092—dc23   2013019125

First Edition
25 24 23 22 21 20 19 18 • 14 13 12 11 10 9 8 7 6

To Mom and Dad:
Your love, challenge, encouragement,
and prayers have marked me and
my leadership forever.
Thank you!

Contents

Foreword

Leadership has been the subject of so many books, studies, and commencement speeches that many people have started to ignore the importance of the message. And, to be fair, authors and speakers often rehash the same clichés and obvious truths, leaving readers and audience members searching for something new.

But maybe it's not something new that we need. Maybe we only need to take a longer, harder look at what we already know but have failed to grasp—the simple but painful truth that if your heart is not right, no one cares about your leadership skills.

In *The Heart of Leadership*, Mark Miller makes a compelling case for a radical form of leadership. According to my dictionary, radical means "favoring extreme changes in existing views, habits, conditions, or institutions." And, Mark's ideas around the heart of leadership just do not correspond to the more self-oriented views, habits, and conditions of today's culture.

This book also illustrates the idea that there is much more to the concept of leadership than most people realize. As the main character in the story comes to understand, wisdom, responsibility, and courage are not generic, fluffy or simplistic concepts that any leader can easily embrace. They can only be achieved through a radical detachment from self, through a painful honesty about our past mistakes and limitations. Anything short of that will leave an aspiring leader, and his or her constituents, feeling empty.

For those who have the courage and the character to embrace the radical nature of heart-based leadership, the rewards are great. But those rewards are not always tangible nor are they guaranteed. They cannot be calculated like a bonus or a 401(k) program. That may be why relatively few leaders choose to lead this way. But perhaps this book will begin to change that. I certainly hope so.

—Patrick Lencioni
President, The Table Group
Author, *The Five Dysfunctions of a Team*
and *The Advantage*

Leadership Character

Have you ever noticed how many books are written to help leaders improve? As many books as there are out there focused on helping leaders enhance their skills, there are far fewer written to help the leader with the all-important self-work—the part on the inside. That's why I'm excited about this book.

I'll let you in on a little discussed fact about leadership: As important as the skills are, lack of skills is not what derails most leaders; skills are too easy to learn. If you want to predict people's ultimate success as leaders, evaluate not their skills but their **leadership character**.

The challenge of growing our leadership character is complicated by a lack of clarity as to what we're actually discussing when the term is used. Ask people what character traits they look for in leaders, and I'm guessing they will probably name attributes like integrity, honesty, and, perhaps, loyalty. These alone are not a great answer. Don't get me wrong—these are fine traits, but they are totally inadequate when describing leadership character.

The best leaders must certainly be honest and have integrity, but we expect these qualities from everyone in our organizations. There are additional traits that set leaders apart. This book is about identifying and developing leadership character. When these traits are evident—and a leader possesses the requisite leadership skills—you find people eager to follow.

So, why is a book like this necessary? This book is intended to help leaders and aspiring leaders strengthen their leadership character, and, as a consequence, position themselves for greater opportunity, influence, and impact. For some of you, the ideas in this book may help transform your leadership and unlock opportunities as you've never imagined. It might even change your life.

If you and I can embrace and cultivate the leadership character traits outlined in this simple story and master the skills needed to lead, our organizations will soar. It will require both—character and skills. Let's begin the hard part today: leadership character first.

Leaders Are Different

"Leaders are different," Samantha said.

"That's it?" Blake said in a tone that revealed his concern.

"Yes, Blake. Your performance has been outstanding; you're a great individual contributor, but I couldn't get enough support for you to become the team leader."

"That doesn't make sense to me," said Blake, in disbelief. "Outstanding performance—no promotion."

"That's right. We do value results around here—but there's something missing." Samantha stopped.

Blake leaned across the table, waiting on her next words, but she said nothing.

He finally broke the silence, "What's missing?" He wanted to know—he needed to know.

"It's really hard for me to put it into words," she said hesitantly. "That's why I said leaders are different."

"Can you tell me how leaders are different?" Blake asked.

"I'm not sure how to describe it, but I know it when I see it." Samantha sounded uncertain.

"Samantha, are you trying to tell me that I'll never get a promotion?" Blake wasn't sure he even wanted the answer to that question.

"No, Blake, I'm not. However, there is a lot more to leadership than great individual work . . . you're just not *acting* like a leader," she said, in a genuine attempt to help.

There is a lot more to leadership than great individual work.

"How do I act like a leader?" Blake's frustration was starting to show.

"Leaders are different."

"Yes, I got that." Blake was hanging on Samantha's every word. He waited, but Samantha didn't seem to have anything else to say. Blake decided one final question was in order: "Do you have any advice for me?"

"You need to figure this out for yourself. You know a lot of leaders; why don't you talk to some of them and see if they can help?"

Samantha wasn't totally satisfied with her response, but she hoped Blake would take her counsel. He did seem to have a lot of potential.

. . .

As Blake drove home, he replayed the previous five years at Dynastar in his head. He felt as if he'd gotten off to a

fast start, maybe the fastest start in history. He had prac-
tically saved the company in his first year—single-hand-
edly. But since then, he had moved three times within
the company and been passed over twice for leadership
positions. He was only 28 years old, but he felt much
older. He was tired. He was stuck. And now he had to
tell Megan.

As he pulled in the driveway, he thought, I wish we
didn't have such a big house payment, then this promotion and the raise wouldn't seem so important. He also
hoped that Megan was in a good mood. Maybe she had
gotten a nap today.

As he entered the house, Clint, their nine-month old,
was screaming about something. None of them had been
sleeping much, and Megan didn't look like she'd had a
nap.

"How are you?" Blake asked, mustering as much of a
smile as he could.

"Okay," Megan said, "I'm tired." As she spoke, she
stepped into the light.

"Have you been crying?" he asked.

"A little."

"Why?"

"The doctor called—" She stopped.

"And . . . ?" Blake probed.

"I'm pregnant!" Megan burst into tears.

"Great," Blake said, with little emotion.

"Great? You're never home, we don't sleep, and we can
hardly pay the bills. What's great about another child?"

The part about "hardly pay the bills" hit Blake like an arrow to his heart. He decided to let it go even though it hurt him deeply.

"Listen," he said. "Another child is a wonderful gift! We'll sleep again someday. And I'll make more money— someday. And about my never being home, I'll keep working on that part, too."

He paused and then said, "I'm thankful we're having another baby. We always talked about having another one."

"We were going to do that later," she sobbed.

"It will be okay." Blake hugged Megan as tightly as he ever had.

When she stopped crying, he said, "You go lie down and take a quick nap. I'll take care of Clint and fix us something to eat. I'll call you in an hour."

"Thank you" was all that Megan could say, as she shuffled off to the bedroom. A nap was the greatest gift Blake could have given her in that moment.

An hour later, much had changed, or at least it felt like it. Clint was happy, Megan was a little more rested and relaxed, and Blake had made a wonderful dinner— well, he had cooked a frozen pizza.

When Megan came back into the kitchen, she said, "I'm sorry I was so emotional earlier. You're right, we do want another child, and there's probably never a good time." She smiled, "Plus, the stress that comes with not sleeping makes everything look more monumental than it really is."

"Here's what I know," Blake added. "It will be great! It may be bumpy, but it will be good." Megan had always loved Blake's optimism.

"How was work today?" Megan asked.

"Well . . . " Blake really didn't want to go there. The timing seemed extremely bad. "It was fine," he said.

"Uh-oh," Meagan said. Blake was not a good liar. "You do still have a job, don't you?"

"Certainly. What would make you think I don't have a job?" Blake was thankful he did still have a job; perhaps that would make the next part easier.

"I do have a job. I don't have a promotion," he said in a matter-of-fact tone.

"I'm sorry, dear." Megan could feel his pain. "What'd they say?"

"I do great work . . . "

"Yes, but?"

"But leaders are different."

"What does that mean?" Megan asked.

"I don't really know. I've only had a couple of hours to think about it. I think they're telling me I'm not a leader."

"You've always been one before." Megan instinctively came to Blake's defense.

"Yes, I know. But Dynastar seems to have a different standard of leadership. I'm still trying to figure it out."

"What are you going to do?"

"Three things," Blake said. "Keep working hard. Keep trying to grow, and I'm going to call Debbie Brewster."

"You do all that," Megan said, "and I'll pray." She smiled; Blake didn't.

When the Student Is Ready

The next morning Clint was up early, so Blake was up early also. While he drank his coffee, he thought about how much Debbie Brewster had helped him after his dad died. He still found it amazing that his dad had mentored Debbie years earlier when she was a struggling leader and then she had then become his mentor.

He credited Debbie with helping him get his job at Dynastar by coaching him through the entire process. She had taught him so much about growing as a leader. He wasn't sure where he'd gotten off track. He was also not sure why he ever stopped meeting with her in the first place. He hoped that she could help him again.

On his way to the office, he gave her a call. Fortunately, but not surprisingly, she was eager to meet with him.

"You name the time and place," Debbie said.

"How about our old spot at the coffee shop?" Blake said.

"Fantastic. When?"

"Tomorrow morning, early?" said Blake. He didn't think he should schedule a meeting in the evening; he knew Megan needed his help at home.

"Great. See you tomorrow morning at 7:00," Debbie said. "What's the topic?"

"I want to talk about how leaders are different."

"I'm glad you asked," Debbie said. Blake sensed she was smiling as she said it. "I'll see you there."

. . .

The morning of the meeting it felt as if the clock had turned back five years. Blake arrived ten minutes early only to find Debbie already seated at a table in the back.

"It's great to see you again!" Blake said, as Debbie stood.

"I was going to say the same thing," Debbie replied. "How are you?"

"Good. I'm married, with a child and another one on the way."

"Really? Congratulations!"

"I can't believe it's been five years. Why did we ever stop meeting?" Blake asked.

"We were both busy. And then John got sick."

"How is he?"

"He died twelve months ago."

"I'm so sorry." Blake couldn't believe he didn't even know.

"Well, that's another reason you and I lost touch. When we got his diagnosis, we decided to travel. We went around the world—it was amazing! We saw things together that made his final months extremely meaningful for both of us. We were married almost thirty years. Marrying him was the best decision I ever made."

"I'm so sorry," Blake repeated. "I'd like to have been there with you at the end."

"It's okay; we've been blessed with many friends."

"I'm glad we've reconnected. You're my only real mentor, and I've missed you."

"Thanks for that compliment, Blake. We'll work hard to stay in touch, but you know you probably need several mentors in your life. But we can talk more about that later. When you called, you said you wanted to discuss how leaders are different."

"Yes," Blake said. "I really need to know."

"What brought this up?"

Blake took the next few minutes to share his story from the previous five years. Debbie listened and took a few notes.

"So, after you served on the cross-functional team, what happened to your supervisor? I think her name was Maggie?"

"She ultimately left the business. She decided to go to work for a nonprofit organization. I wanted her job, but I didn't get it. That was the first time I was passed over for a leadership position."

"And it happened again yesterday?" Debbie was trying to get the facts straight.

"Yes, that's when Samantha told me leaders are different. I didn't know what to do with that, so I called you."

"Okay, I think I've got the context. Specifically, how can I help?"

"You tell me. I'm frustrated, confused, and stuck!" Blake said.

"Okay, first, let me tell you that you *can* be a leader. I've known it since you were 16 years old," Debbie said, reassuringly.

"I'm glad you think so—no one else seems to."

"Your dad thought so, too."

"I know. That's just one more reason this whole thing is so painful." Blake paused and looked at the floor. "You know, in the last conversation we ever had, he told me I could be a leader. I didn't believe him then, and I'm not too sure I believe him today."

"Listen, Blake, here's the reality of the situation. You're 28 years old. You were not passed over for Maggie's job. You weren't seasoned, proven, or, quite frankly, qualified. You weren't a viable candidate."

No one had ever been so direct on this issue before. He didn't know what to say. When he started to speak, Debbie stopped him.

"No, let me finish. However, you may have been passed over yesterday. But that's great news! It sounds like the wake-up call you needed."

"Wake-up call? What do you mean?"

"Listen, Samantha was correct—leaders *are* different. And I'm thankful we're having this conversation now when you're 28 rather than waiting until you are 58. If you can figure this out now, you can lead for the rest of your life. And finally, do not associate leadership with a position. You can lead, with or without, a title. If you wait until you get a title, you could wait forever."

Debbie wasn't finished, "You led early in your career at Dynastar without a position of leadership. Why did you stop?"

"I'm not sure. The truth of the matter is I didn't realize I had stopped leading. But I'm ready to get back in the game," Blake said, opening his notebook. "Where do we start?"

You can lead, with or without, a title.
If you wait until you get a title,
you could wait forever.

"Give me a napkin," Debbie said.

"Another treasure map?" Blake said, remembering the last time Debbie drew on a napkin for him.

"Nothing that elaborate," she smiled. "Did you and I ever talk about icebergs?"

"No, we talked about my getting a job; we talked about what I needed to do to *grow* as a leader; no . . . no recollection of an iceberg. I think I would remember that," Blake grinned.

"This is something else your dad taught me. The iceberg is a perfect picture of leadership. Think back to grade school; about how much of the iceberg is above the water?"

"Ten percent?" Blake thought that was correct.

"Yes, and the balance is below the water. It's the same with leaders—10 percent above the waterline and about 90 percent below. Your dad taught me about *both*."

"The part above the water represents **leadership skills.** The part below represents **leadership character,**" Debbie finished her sentence and her drawing simultaneously.

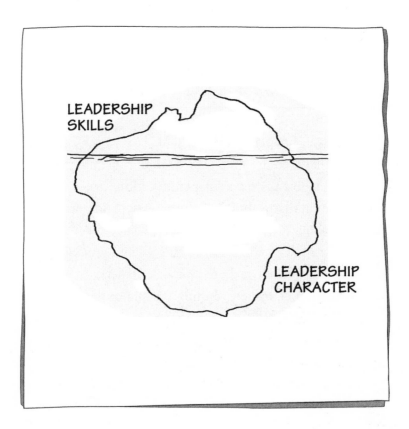

"So?" Blake wasn't sure how this spoke to leaders being different.

"So," Debbie continued, "skills represent things leaders do. You and I talked about skills quite a lot a few years ago."

"Yes, I remember—I've been working on that."

"Outstanding." Debbie, true to her nature, was very affirming.

She continued, "The balance of the iceberg, the part under the water, represents leadership character. Ninety percent of our success as leaders will be determined by what's below the waterline. It's our leadership character that ultimately drives what we do, and why. It is a true reflection of who we really are as human beings."

"When you say it like that, it sounds really important."

"More than you can imagine," Debbie added.

"Can you give me an example?" Blake asked.

"Sure. If you help Megan with the dishes, what does she think?"

"She thinks I'm amazing," he chuckled.

"Not so fast. If you help her because you feel obligated to help her or if you want something in return, you'll not get the credit you think you deserve. However, if you serve her because *you want* to serve her—no strings attached—*then* she'll think you're great. Same action—totally different outcome."

"Does she really know *why* I'm serving her?" Blake asked sheepishly.

"Absolutely," Debbie said, without flinching.

"And the difference?" Blake stopped.

"The difference is your motivation—your character—your heart. What's below the waterline colors everything we *do* as a leader. We cannot conceal our heart for long—if at all."

"I think I'm tracking with you. So let's go back to how this connects with the idea leaders are different," Blake said.

"What comes to mind when I say 'character'?"

"Honesty, integrity, loyalty—things like that."

"Okay, those are outstanding attributes or qualities, but they are not unique to leaders. They are not distinctives."

"What do you mean?"

"You want every person in your organization to be honest, demonstrate integrity, and be loyal."

"Sure," Blake agreed.

"But, that's not what makes leaders different. The men and women who lead, at least those who lead well, certainly have the traits you mentioned, but they also have other traits that set them apart."

"Is that what my supervisor means when she says leaders are different?"

"I can't be sure, but my guess is yes. Regardless, you need to understand this concept; it will affect your leadership for the rest of your life."

"This sounds bigger than I thought. I was just trying to get to the next level at Dynastar. I'm not sure I'm ready to talk about the rest of my life," Blake said sheepishly.

"That's exactly what we're talking about—the rest of your life as a leader." Debbie offered this with a firm yet warm stare.

"Leadership character is the primary driver of your success as a leader."

"What about skills?" Blake asked.

"They are important, but the lack of skills is not what derails most leaders—skills are too easy to learn. It is ultimately leadership character that determines our opportunity for influence and impact."

"Okay, and?" Blake said with a question in his voice.

"Let me say it again, when leaders fail to thrive, the culprit is often their leadership character, not their lack of skills."

"I think I should be offended at this point," Blake said. "You're questioning my character?"

"No, let me say it differently; stay with me," Debbie continued. "You can have impeccable character—be honest, loyal, dependable, and so on—and still not demonstrate *leadership character*."

"So this is not about being loyal, dependable, having integrity, and other admirable traits like that?" Blake was trying to put all of this together.

"Of course you need those traits. But they are not enough. Leadership character sits on top of the character traits you just mentioned—integrity, loyalty, and other traits like them are foundational. Leaders who don't possess these are disqualified before they start. Successful leaders demonstrate additional qualities—the traits of leadership character—in their day-to-day efforts to lead. If you don't demonstrate leadership character, your skills and your results will be discounted, if not dismissed."

"How can results be dismissed?"

"If people don't see you demonstrating leadership character, they won't see you as a leader, no matter how great your results. People will just see you as a talented individual contributor. Great to have on the team, but they won't let you call any of the plays. They won't ever let you lead."

"Okay . . . " Blake paused, trying to figure out his next question. "So if I don't have leadership character, am I doomed as a leader?"

---

*If you don't demonstrate leadership
character, your skills and your results
will be discounted, if not dismissed.*

"Certainly not. That's not what I've been trying to say. What I do need to tell you is that forming, transforming, or reforming character is difficult—extremely difficult—but it is possible."

"So how do I develop leadership character?" Blake demonstrated his usual energy and drive.

"First, you've got to be clear on what leadership character looks like in action."

"Can you just tell me? It sounds like you know exactly what leadership character looks like."

"I could tell you, but I've got a better idea. Here's what I'm going to ask you to do. Your dad was part of a small group that met on a regular basis."

"Yes, I know. They met for years."

"They still do." Debbie added, "I'm going to give you their names and contact information. All you need to do is schedule a meeting with each one and ask them to talk with you about leadership character. They'll be excited to meet you."

"Are you sure they'll meet with me? I'm guessing if they were in Dad's small group, they're probably busy people."

"Yes, they'll meet with you. Tell them I suggested the meeting. That's all you'll have to say."

It's Not About You

When Blake got to his office, he already had an email from Debbie with the names of the men and women in his father's former group. Judging from their titles alone, it looked like an eclectic group—a CEO, a judge, the leader of a large nonprofit, a high school football coach, and a school superintendent.

Blake started making calls and scheduling meetings. He was delighted that everyone he called seemed genuinely interested in meeting with him.

His first meeting was in about a week.

. . .

Monday morning at 7:00, Blake found himself standing on the curb in front of an old building in the heart of the city. He was not alone; a couple of dozen other people waited for the doors to open as well. As Blake looked at his watch, he had a sense that no one else in the group was concerned about the time. Although he was attempting not to be judgmental, he assumed, based on their appearance, that his companions on the curb were all homeless. The crowd had gathered at Heaven's Kitchen, a nonprofit organization started by Chad Culpepper. Chad was the youngest member of his dad's small group. He had joined right out of college.

At about 7:05, the doors opened. Blake and the others made their way into a large room with long tables. The men and women who'd been waiting formed a line at one end of the room. They seemed to know the routine.

Blake watched as people went through the line, picking up what looked like oatmeal and a piece of toast. At the end—where you would expect a cash register to be— each guest was greeted by a young man. Although Blake couldn't hear what was being said, he noticed that the conversations were brief; they all seemed to begin with a handshake and end with a hug.

After watching for about five minutes, Blake realized he should probably be looking for Chad. He approached one of the hostesses in the dining room.

"Hi, I'm looking for Chad." The woman pointed to the man at the end of the line. He was the one everyone talked to before they sat down to eat.

Just then, Chad caught Blake's eye and motioned him over. Chad was standing there with a man who appeared to be about 80 years old. Blake knew it was probably just life on the street that had aged his appearance.

Chad spoke first as Blake approached, "You must be Blake. Thanks for coming by. I want you to meet someone. This is Larry. Larry, this is Blake. Blake is Jeff Brown's son."

"Jeff Brown was the finest man I ever knew," Larry said.

Blake was flabbergasted. "You knew my dad?"

"Knew him? He was my hero. He used to stand right here where Chad is standing today. He established the handshake and the hug ritual. He taught us—no, he showed us—that we mattered regardless of our circumstances. He showed us honor, dignity, and respect . . . and he loved us."

Blake just stood there, literally speechless.

Chad broke the awkward silence. "Larry's had some hard times, but he's making it. He works several days a week now. He's also been in school recently learning to be a mechanic."

"One more semester." Larry smiled.

"We're here just to help him get by until he can get back on his feet. Thanks for coming in today, Larry."

"Thank you, Chad." Larry gave Chad a hug and turned and hugged Blake also.

Blake was still trying to get his bearings. He was feeling overwhelmed. The place, the people, the need, the hugs, the fact Larry knew his dad. It was all a bit too much in the moment.

Chad said, "Let's have a seat." He motioned to someone else who took over his spot at the end of the line.

The handshake and hug would continue to be part of every guest's visit.

"Thanks for coming today, Blake."

"Larry knew my dad," Blake said, still trying to process what he'd just learned.

"Yes, many of the men and women in here this morning knew your dad."

"How did they know him?" Blake asked.

"He used to come here a lot. As Larry said, he stood right there giving out handshakes and hugs."

"I didn't know. How could I not know?"

"Your dad didn't come here for attention; he came here to give it. Maybe that's why he didn't tell you."

"Wow. I knew my dad was a great leader, but this is a side of him I didn't know about."

"Maybe you're getting an insight into why he was a great leader," Chad added. "Now, why did you want to meet today?"

"Oh, yes, I'm trying to strengthen my leadership character. Debbie Brewster suggested I meet with you."

"I love these meetings!" Chad's energy level picked up a level. "Before we proceed, who else have you met with?"

"You're the first on my list."

"I love being first."

"Why?"

"Because I think what I've got to say is the most important."

"Really? Why is what you have to share with me most important?"

"Has someone drawn the iceberg for you?"

"Yes, Debbie did."

"Great, we'll skip that. But you remember, leadership is both what's above the waterline—"

"The skills," Blake interjected.

"Yes, the skills—but the majority of leadership is what's below the waterline. That's what you're trying to learn about—leadership character. It's the game changer. Your ultimate success will not be determined by your level of skills. Leaders rarely fail because of lack of skills. They're too easy to learn. It's leadership character that trips up a lot of leaders.

"So your challenge and mine is to understand, embrace, and cultivate both the leadership character and the skills needed to lead."

"That's sounds like a great summary of what Debbie's been trying to help me understand." This conversation was already helping Blake get clarity on the challenge ahead. Now he just needed some of the specifics about this thing called leadership character.

"Okay, so what do you believe is the most important element of leadership character?"

"**Think others first**," Chad said.

Blake jotted down Chad's comment.

"Exactly what does that mean to you?" Blake wanted to be clear on the implications.

Facets of Leadership Character

Think Others First

"In my opinion, this is what really separates the best leaders from everyone else. If you miss this one, you'll struggle with all the other things you're going to learn on your visits about leadership character . . . and you'll never be a great servant leader."

"Now, I did hear my dad talk about servant leadership. To tell you the truth, I don't think I was listening too well. I was just a kid, and I was not thinking about serving others. I was mostly focused on me and my life."

"That's understandable. And I think your choice of words is insightful. Many leaders stumble because they never get past that point."

"Which point?" Blake asked.

"The point where they are completely focused on their life, their career, their agenda, and their recognition. I'm glad you're here today. You're still young. Your greatest leadership impact can still lie in your future."

"I'm glad to be here, too. Let's go back to this idea of servant leadership. I have a couple of questions—first, what is it, exactly?"

"Servant leadership is an approach contrary to conventional leadership in which the leader's focus is on himself and what he can accomplish and achieve. Rather, the focus is on those being served. Servant leaders do many of the same things other leaders do—cast vision, build teams, allocate resources, and so on. The big difference is their orientation and their motivation; these make all the difference in the world. They possess an others-first mindset. The servant leader constantly works to help others win."

"Can't you lead without being a servant leader?"

"Sure you can. But in most settings, traditional leadership is outdated. It relies too heavily on the contribution of the leader and undervalues the talent and skills of those being led. The best leaders want to leverage all the capabilities of the people in their organization. I don't want to get stuck with old, antiquated methods. Servant leadership is a higher form of leadership. Servant leadership is the path to superior, sustained results."

"Why does servant leadership work so well?"

"Servant leadership works for many reasons: First, it focuses on others—specifically, those you desire to lead. Your ever-present question is not what can you do for yourself; rather, it is how can you serve them? When decisions are made, you consider the organization and your people before you weigh the personal consequences.

"Servant leadership also works because it honors people—being a servant leader acknowledges the different roles, responsibilities, and strengths of people. It is not about who's in charge. It's about who is responsible for what, and how can I, as the leader, help people be successful?

"Another reason it works so well is servant leadership builds trust—we trust leaders whose motives are others-centered. Candor, feedback, encouragement, and even directives feel different when trust is present. When our leaders serve, we trust them more. Trust is also a key ingredient in loyalty and retention.

The servant leader constantly works to help others win.

"Next, it raises engagement—there is clearly an inspirational component at play when we see our leaders serve on our behalf. It energizes us as followers. When you and I believe that our leaders are for us and that they want to serve us, we want to serve them and the organizations they lead.

"And finally, leadership always reveals the heart of the leader—even when what is exposed is not pretty. If it is a heart focused on serving together to accomplish a common goal, it motivates people to do their best work. The sense that we're doing this together makes servant leadership extremely powerful."

"Wow! It sounds like you've thought about this," Blake said, as he frantically tried to capture some of what he'd just heard in his notes.

"I have. I did my thesis on servant leadership. Did you know we graduated from the same school?"

"No, I didn't."

"Yep, I was about five years ahead of you. When I graduated, I needed to decide what to do with my life. That's when I met Debbie and your dad. They helped me more than I can describe. They taught me that at the end of the day, what matters most is what I've done to serve others. That's how our lives will be evaluated. Not by the things we amassed. Don't get me wrong, there's nothing wrong with stuff. But, what we do for others matters most."

"That's why you said the most important character trait for a leader is think others first."

"Yes, that's why. For me, that means starting this place. For your dad, it meant making a lot of money so he could help even more people than I could ever imagine. The ways we impacted people's lives were different, but we both had the same motivation—we wanted to serve. We consider serving others a high calling."

"Okay, I think I understand. What I need to know is how to get off my own agenda. How do I think others first if that's not my natural bent?"

"First, don't feel all alone. My experience is that most leaders could ask the same question—I struggle, too."

"You do? You run a nonprofit to feed homeless people! What could be more others-centered?"

"Let me offer a clarification. To think others first is not primarily about what you do—it is about how you think. Think others first, as with the other facets of leadership character you're going to discover, is all about what's in your heart, not what you do with your hands."

"So how do I do it, think others first?"

"I have a couple of ideas, but no guarantees."

"I'm not looking for guarantees; I'm looking for ideas that work," Blake said with a faint smile.

"Here are a few things I do to help me think others first.

"I intentionally cultivate relationships with servant leaders. Debbie is one of them. Your father was another. It always amazes me how much you can learn by spending time with people. I've always heard you become like your friends. If you hang out with folks who run marathons, chances are good you'll run one, too. If you hang out with bookworms, you'll read more, and so on."

"Funny you say that, three of the people on my team have run marathons, and I'm training for my first one."

"See, that's how it works. I want to be a better servant leader, so I try to be sure I'm in that circle as much as possible. That's why I was so thankful when your dad invited me to join his group. Every time we meet, I feel stronger as a leader, regardless of the topic we discuss."

"It makes sense. I believe we do become like those we associate with." Blake made a note to himself.

"That association has other value," Chad continued.

"Like what?"

"By hanging around serving leaders, I can see how they act and begin to figure out how they think. Then, in my normal day-to-day reality, I can ask myself, what would a great servant leader do? My answer is then informed by my experience and observations.

"You'd be surprised how often that simple question affects my behavior. After a recent fund-raising event, I started to leave, but then I asked myself the question: What would a great servant leader do? My answer: I found all the members of the hotel staff who served us during the evening and thanked them for their hard work and excellent service. Was that a major deal? No, but it felt like a "think others first" kind of thing to do. My days are full of those examples. Over time, I find I don't have to ask the question as often."

"Why not?"

"I think my heart is changing."

"That's sounds like a big deal."

"I think so. And it makes sense to me. The heart is a muscle, and you strengthen muscles by using them. The more I lead with my heart, the stronger it gets."

"I'm getting the feeling my heart needs a workout. I'm certainly not where I need to be on this issue.

"I'm glad you see its importance. If your heart doesn't change, leadership character will always be a struggle for you."

"Did you say you had another suggestion?"

"One more—just serve."

"Serve?"

"Yes. Look for as many ways as possible to serve people."

"How?"

"Anyway you can."

"Help me here. I'm not sure I'm following you."

"If you go through life looking for ways to serve others, you'll be focused on others. That's what think others first is all about. It's about getting the focus off ourselves. Serving leaders don't think less of themselves, they just think of themselves less."

"Won't people take advantage of you?"

"What do you mean?"

"Well, if people get the idea that I'll serve them . . . they may want me to serve them."

"What an opportunity!"

"Really?"

"Yes. You'll still have to have appropriate boundaries, but at the heart of being a servant leader is serving others. When we get the chance, that's what we love to do! And, the best part, organizations will pay us to do it. Even here, in a nonprofit organization, they pay me to serve."

"That doesn't sound very strategic—just serve."

"It's not strategic in a traditional sense. However, serving in the day-to-day prepares your heart to serve in the more strategic fashion you typically associate with leaders."

"I'd like to learn about that."

"That's another topic for another day. Besides, Debbie is the real expert on this topic."

"Can you at least tell me what you mean when you say 'more strategic' ways leaders serve?"

"Sure, your dad taught me. It's kind of cool to pass it on to you. Remember the iceberg?"

"Yes."

"Okay, the 10 percent above the waterline—"

"The skills?" Blake jumped in.

"Yes, the skills can be summarized in five strategic ways great leaders **SERVE**.

They are:

See the Future

Engage and Develop Others

Reinvent Continuously

Value Results and Relationships

Embody the Values"

When Chad finished, Blake just sat there looking at his notes.

Finally, Blake broke the silence, "My dad taught you this?"

"Yes, and more importantly, he showed me. He was a good man."

"I know. I want to be like him," Blake said in a moment of total transparency.

"Don't try."

"What do you mean?"

"He wouldn't want you to be like him, he'd want you to be like you," Chad said.

"You're right." Blake's words didn't mask his desire to be more like his dad.

"Here's my encouragement for you. Focus on what we've talked about today. The five practices we just reviewed are critical, but they are secondary. If you don't demonstrate leadership character, the practices are irrelevant."

"This has been extremely helpful. Any closing thoughts?" Blake asked.

"Just one," Chad began. "The more you serve the more likely you are to develop a think others first mind-set. It will change you more than you can imagine. It will soften your heart. You will be a better leader and a better person. The ability to think others first is the foundation of leadership character. Don't miss it."

"I'll try not to," Blake said.

"You probably need to get to the office, and I need to start getting ready for lunch. Lots of handshakes and hugs needed in the world today. Thanks for coming!"

. . .

Later that evening when Blake arrived home, he spent
about an hour trying to explain his visit with Chad to
Megan. Although he had taken great notes, he was having
trouble explaining the effect the meeting had on him.

"I can't seem to articulate what I'm feeling," he said.

"It sounds like it was an emotional visit," Megan
suggested.

"Yes, I guess it was. When Larry said my dad was his
hero, then Chad told me Dad was a regular volunteer
there, I was a wreck for the rest of the conversation. I've
got some huge shoes to fill."

"I think that's a big part of your problem," Megan
said. "You know I love you, but you've not been the same
since your dad died. It's not that you've been bad, just different. I think you're trying to be something you can't be.
You can't be him. Today just made the challenge even bigger in your mind. Let's face it—the man was a saint." She
smiled a warm smile, paused, and said, "You're good, but
you're no saint!" They both laughed.

"I think you're pushing. You've been pushing. You're
measuring your life, and our life, against your dad's life
and his accomplishments. That's probably why we have
this house we don't need and can't afford. It's probably
why you've been too self-focused versus others-focused at
the office. It's probably why when you were 23 you were
mentoring kids and why you stopped when your career
became 'too' demanding."

"Let me say it again: I love you. I'm with you—for better or worse, sickness or health, and all of it. But the Blake I fell in love with is the better man. That man wasn't trying to be his father. If you'll be you, I think you'll be fine."

This was the second time that day Blake was speechless. He had no idea Megan felt this way. While he sat there in silence, she continued.

"Maybe it's because I'm pregnant, I don't know. Maybe it's my hormones or something. I just think you are amazing. You, trying to be someone else—not as amazing."

He wondered if he just sat there if she'd continue. He decided not to take that chance. "I'm sorry."

"Don't be sorry . . . be you."

Hearing Megan's admonition, Blake had a flashback to the advice he'd received from Chad earlier in the day.

"How about an improved version of me?"

"Improved? What do you have in mind?"

"Well, I appreciate your kind and candid words, but you're also biased. You love me."

"I'm glad we have that established."

"Me too!" Blake smiled. "However, I think you've chosen to overlook some of my shortcomings."

"Yes, I have."

"Well, moving into the future, I want to be a better version of myself."

"Give me an example."

"As I'm learning about leadership character, I want to cultivate those traits. Not to be more like my dad but to be a better father, husband, employee, and leader. Today, I learned something I can work on."

"Like what?" Now Megan was really curious.

"Think others first for a start. I can do better on this, for sure."

"You have my full support. Just don't push. Think back to your skiing days. What inevitably happened when you would push?"

"I would lose the race."

"No, more specifically, what happened?"

"I usually crashed," Blake admitted.

"Exactly. And when you crashed back then it was bad. I remember you almost died once. But now you've got to think about us. You have a family—a family that loves you. Don't push—don't crash."

"I promise. Now, let me tell you about Larry."

Leaders Create the Future

Blake's next meeting was scheduled for a week later. He would be meeting with Joe Conrad. Joe was the CEO of a global pharmaceutical company. Blake did some pre-work by researching Joe's company. He was impressed. It was huge—one of the largest of its kind in the world. They had a proven track record of industry leadership and innovation. Blake was excited to be meeting with Mr. Conrad.

On the morning of the meeting, Blake arrived early and was thankful for the extra time. He had not anticipated the high security at the facility. When he finally made it to the building, he was stunned. It was by far the nicest office building he'd ever seen. The furniture, the fixtures, the design, the artwork. Blake was almost positive one of the paintings on the wall was one he had studied in college in an art history course. He was careful not to break anything.

Just as he was taking one last look around the lobby, a woman approached him: "Mr. Conrad will see you now," she said. She escorted him into a large office. Joe came from around his desk to greet him.

"Welcome! I'm so glad you called." Joe offered his hand and a huge smile.

"Thank you for seeing me, sir. As I told your assistant, I have just one question for you."

"Have a seat, Blake. We'll get to your question, but I've got several for you."

Without leadership character, no one cares about your skills.

For the next thirty minutes, Joe asked Blake about his mom, his career, his hopes and dreams, and more. It was a bit overwhelming. Blake was glad Joe was interested in his life, but he wanted to ask *his* question. However, he waited patiently and did his best to answer all of Joe's questions.

"Okay, thanks for helping me catch up. What's your question?" Joe asked.

"Debbie Brewster has been mentoring me on and off for several years. Do you know Debbie?"

"Yes, very well. She's a gifted leader and a great coach."

"She's been an outstanding coach for me," Blake said. "She suggested that I come to see you."

"And she wanted you to ask me about the character traits of a leader—am I right?"

"Yes, sir, how did you know?"

"You're not the first, but that doesn't matter. What matters is that I have an answer for you."

"That's why I'm here. What have you got for me?"
Blake smiled.

"Did she tell you why leadership character matters?"

"She said without leadership character, people won't see me as a leader."

"That's true. I've got my own way to say that:

"Without leadership character, no one cares about your skills."

Blake made a note. Then he said, "That sounds harsh."

"The truth is often harsh," Joe said in a quiet tone.

"If I grow my leadership skills and strengthen my leadership character, will I always be given leadership opportunities?"

"When you say 'given leadership opportunities,' do you mean a promotion?" Joe sought clarification.

"I have been trying to get one." As Blake responded, he knew it wasn't the right answer.

"No, it doesn't work like that. Don't confuse opportunity with leadership. Others control many of our opportunities, so that shouldn't be our concern. We control our readiness.

"Here's an example outside the world of work. When my son was four or five years old he started playing baseball. He was in the outfield. He told me he wanted to play in the infield. I told him to be ready—he might get a chance someday.

"One day, during a game, they put him in the infield. Do you know what happened?"

"What?"

"The first batter hit a ground ball right at him, he didn't even have to move, but he missed it; it went right under his glove."

"What did the coach do?"

"The very next inning, he was moved back in the outfield."

"I know he hated that."

"He did. We talked about it on the way home. He shared his frustration. I told him to get ready. I didn't know if the coach would ever put him back in the infield. But if he did, he'd want to be able to catch ground balls. It's a big part of what infielders do, you know."

"And?" The athlete in Blake was rooting for Joe's son.

"He practiced and practiced, and in a few weeks the coach put him back in the infield."

"And?" Blake asked.

"He played in the infield for the next twenty years— played on a college team and had offers to play in the minor leagues. All of that was predicated on him doing what he could do. He had to get ready. So do you and I."

"Before we move on, I want to encourage you. Although it is true that others control many of our leadership opportunities, in my experience, the world is starving for the right kind of leaders. If you and I prepare ourselves—both our skills and our leadership character— there will be ample opportunities to lead."

"One more thing—these last few minutes brought a question to mind. You do know you don't need a formal title, position, or invitation to lead, don't you?"

"Yes, sir, that's a subject Debbie and I have discussed often."

"My challenge to you: Get ready to lead and opportunities to lead will not be your problem."

"That brings us back to the question of the day. How do you recognize leadership character? I'm guessing Debbie has asked you to make several visits."

"Yes, sir."

"Who've you met with so far?"

"Just Chad Culpepper."

"Outstanding young leader," Joe offered. "Okay then, I'll just share one trait with you today and let the others on your journey share additional ones. Here's my contribution—**expect the best**."

Blake wrote it in his notes.

Facets of Leadership Character

Think Others First

Expect the Best

"Please tell me more," Blake said.

"Blake, you know the world is full of challenges. All you have to do is watch the news, and you could get the feeling that the world is hopeless."

"Yeah, it's pretty bad. If it's not the economy, there's a drought or a flood or a war."

"Or some combination of all the above," Joe added.

"Many people in the world see events as they are; leaders are different in that they see things that could be. And the future they see is always a better version of the present. We believe we can make a difference; we think we can make the world, or at least our part of it, better. Leaders are generally more optimistic than nonleaders.

"To expect the best is an attitude, a belief, a choice, a lifestyle and a trait that virtually every successful leader possesses. We believe the best about others and about ourselves."

"How has this affected your leadership?" Blake asked.

"We're a pharmaceutical company. We create new drugs. Our batting average is lousy. Only a fraction of the new drugs we test will become commercially viable, and they cost billions to create."

"Why do you do it?"

"Because we make the world a better place! That one-in-a-thousand drug can save lives! We are in the lifesaving business. We can't focus on our failures; we must focus on our successes—especially those that have yet to come to fruition. I couldn't lead this enterprise successfully if I was a pessimist.

"Expect the best! You won't always get it, but that outlook will make you a better leader. Who wants to follow a pessimist?" Joe asked rhetorically. "Not me. Maybe other pessimists, but I doubt it. Napoleon said, 'Leaders are dealers in hope.' Hope of a better tomorrow. How can you be a dealer in hope if you don't believe in a better tomorrow?"

"Is there a risk in expecting the best?" Blake asked.

"Absolutely. There's risk in everything. When you expect the best, one of the risks is that you'll not be grounded in reality. However, optimism is not about ignoring the facts. You still need the facts. You also need people around you to tell you the truth.

"However, there is greater risk in expecting the worst. Pessimists will have trouble attracting followers. They will be timid and avoid risk, and the opportunity and rewards that go with that risk will forever elude the leader."

"How would your life be different if you didn't expect the best?" Blake asked.

"It's hard to say," Joe paused. "I'm sure I wouldn't be leading this company. I probably wouldn't have gone to an Ivy League school, and I wouldn't have married the woman of my dreams."

"Slow down. Help me with all that," Blake said.

"I couldn't lead at the level required of this organization if I didn't expect the best. I already told you about the challenges of our industry. We would never market a new drug if I allowed us to focus on our failures. I wouldn't want to follow me if that were the case." He smiled.

"Next, if I didn't expect the best possible outcome, I wouldn't have applied to any out-of- state schools, much less the Ivy League."

"Why did you?"

"Because I expected the best—I thought I had a chance. I also knew that I really didn't have anything to lose beyond the application fee, some time, and a stamp."

"A stamp?" Blake said.

Joe smiled, "Back in my day, we didn't have the Internet. We mailed things."

"Oh, a postage stamp—I've seen those," Blake grinned. "Sorry, back to your story about your school choice."

"I was turned down by ten schools, and then one said yes, which leads to the woman of my dreams. There are two ways expecting the best made that relationship possible.

"First, we went to the same university. The chances of meeting her would have been highly unlikely if I was at my local junior college, and she was in Boston.

"Second, when I first met her, my friends told me that she was out of my league. They were right, but my optimism led me to ask her out—several times—did I tell you that persistence is another good leadership trait? She finally said yes, and next week we'll celebrate forty-two years of marriage. I'm thankful I expected the best! I'll also say that same attitude has helped my marriage. I'm not perfect, and the truth is neither is my wife. But, one of the gifts we give each other is to expect the best. It's part of why we're still happily married.

I'm sure there are countless other ways my life would be different if I didn't expect the best."

"That's a great story!" said Blake. "But has expecting the best ever created a problem for you as a leader?"

"Sure. I can think of two examples immediately. One, a product issue and the other was a people issue.

"First, the product example: We were developing a new drug—we were trying to. We ran into problem after problem for years. It was costing millions, which isn't that unusual.

"However, my optimism was so strong about this drug, we pushed several years beyond what our normal process called for. I was pushing. I was expecting the best. In the end, I was wrong. It cost us a lot of money.

"Now, the people example. I actually do this more than I want to admit. I have let my "expect the best attitude" keep me from making a tough call related to an individual's future with our company. We work diligently to get the right people on the team. However, we make mistakes. From time to time, we make a bad selection. More than once, expecting the best has slowed the process of correcting a bad hiring decision. I just want to believe that everyone can be successful. My team agrees with that sentiment; however, some people are going to be more successful *outside* our company."

Blake said, "I have one final question. What advice do you have for me to help me expect the best more often?"

Joe began, "I have two suggestions for you.

"First, believe in your ability to create the future. That's what leaders do—that is our job. Understand reality but never be imprisoned by it. Reality is a moment in time. The future has not yet been written—it is written by leaders."

"Can you give me an example?"

"I'll give you two—again, a product example and then a people example.

"First, the product example: We saw a need in the market. There were millions of people suffering from a particular issue. It looked like a strategic opportunity. With the aging of America, not to mention the global market, the potential for this product would be huge. There was only one problem—maybe two. We had no expertise in this particular field. Second, it was rumored, our competitors had been working on this same issue for several years."

The future has not yet been written—
it is written by leaders.

"What happened?" Blake asked.

"I made the call to get in the game. I thought the upside rewards outweighed the risks. And, thanks to the hard work of our team, and perhaps a little luck, we had a breakthrough and were first to market. We made billions." He smiled.

"What if you'd guessed wrong? What if you'd not had a breakthrough?"

"We'd have cut our losses or waited to create the generic products that would follow. But let me address the question behind your question. Expecting the best is not about always being right. It is about a belief in yourself and in your team. There will always be calculated risk in a leader's world. That's a significant part of what we get paid to do—identify the risks worth taking. If you don't expect the best, you'll take few risks. Without risk, you'll always underperform your potential."

Joe continued, "Thankfully, on the people issue, I've got scores of these examples. When you expect the best from people, you will often see more in them than they see in themselves. The good news is that people generally rise to the level of expectations placed on them. So, when you see people with untapped potential and you call them on it, it's a lot of fun to see them thrive."

"One of our success stories is Sally Johnson. She's the head of marketing for us. She started in our call center answering customers' and doctors' questions."

"You're kidding? The head of marketing for a multibillion dollar, global firm started on the help desk?"

"Yes, and had we not challenged her, she would still be in that role. What do you expect of people? That's a big question every leader answers. The best leaders expect the best from people.

"The other bit of advice may be the most important: Choose to be optimistic. Expecting the best is ultimately a way of thinking. You and I choose the way we think. No one else does this for us. We own it."

"Expecting the best is a big deal for leaders," Blake admitted. "I've never thought about it before today."

"Do you have an "expect the best" outlook on life, Blake?" Joe asked.

"I really need to give it some thought, but I think I'm pretty good on this. I always see the glass as half full."

"No, Blake, actually, the glass is always *completely* full—half air and half liquid," Joe smiled.

Blake laughed, "Now, that's a new level of optimism!"

"Yes. That's the way your father saw the glass, too. Your father's choice to expect the best was one of his most defining traits. He always expected the best of us. His optimism inspired us all."

"It inspired me, too. Thanks for your time today. You've been very generous."

"Please call on me any time. I'd love to stay in touch. And tell your mom I said hello."

Vision Fuels Courage

The meeting with Joe had been extremely helpful. Blake was glad that, as best as he could tell, he was doing okay on the "expect the best" front. Would he be so fortunate regarding the other facets of leadership character? He would soon find out.

After his meeting with Joe, Blake was more attentive than ever at the office. He was on the lookout for an expect the best attitude. Where would it show up? In what form? Would he see it at all?

Interestingly enough, when he looked for it, he saw it. He saw it from senior leaders and some of his peers. He even saw it in some of the new interns. Blake knew this ability alone would not make a leader, but it was good to recognize this critical leadership character trait.

Because it was going to be several days before his meeting with Molly, Blake decided to get in touch with Debbie to see if they could meet sooner than scheduled. He was glad she was available.

. . .

"How are things at home?" Debbie asked. "How's Megan feeling?"

"Generally, things are good. Megan's sick almost every morning, but she feels better as the day goes on. I'm working hard to get home early enough in the evening to help around the house. Clint is also sleeping better. I think we're going to make it." He smiled.

"Tell me what you've learned so far."

Blake began, "I've had two outstanding meetings. I met Chad Culpepper and Joe Conrad. They helped me understand leadership character is multifaceted."

Blake stopped and looked at Debbie, "But you already knew that." He smiled wryly.

"So, what I feel like I'm doing is putting together a puzzle. Chad and Joe have given me the first two pieces."

"And they are?" Debbie asked.

"Think others first and expect the best."

"How will these first two traits affect your leadership?"

Blake said, "I'm not sure."

"Do you naturally expect the best?"

He hesitated. "I think so."

"I would agree."

"How about think others first?"

"That's not currently a strength," Blake admitted, "but I'm already working to incorporate some of what Chad shared with me into my daily routine."

"Like what?" Debbie wanted to hear how Blake was applying his new leadership insight.

"As I began to really focus on my behaviors, and more importantly, my attitude, I realized I entered almost every conversation or interaction with the wrong mindset."

"That sounds serious." Debbie added. "Please, tell me more."

"I realized I was always focused on what I wanted or needed, or the idea I was trying to advance."

"And . . . ?" Debbie said.

"And none of that feels like think others first to me."

"Great awareness; what are you going to do about it?"

"I've already started. I'm trying to cultivate the habit of asking myself two questions before every conversation:

"How can I serve this person?"
"What does a win look like for him or her?"

"How's it going so far?"

"It's been fun; especially when I can actually do something to help."

"Please keep me posted on your progress."

"I will." Blake made himself a note. "I'm looking forward to my next meeting. As I said, I've got two pieces of the leadership character puzzle. I'm eager to get the next one."

"Stay in touch!"

. . .

Blake's next meeting would be with Molly Ortega, the school superintendent for their district, one of the largest in the country. She was responsible for more than 100 schools, hundreds of faculty and staff, and, ultimately, for the education of thousands of children. Blake knew enough about education to know that she had ongoing leadership challenges.

When he got to her office, Ms. Ortega's assistant informed him that Molly would arrive shortly, and invited him to look around. Blake noticed the stark difference in the furnishings here and what he had seen at Mr. Conrad's office. This furniture was standard government grade. However, the walls in Ms. Ortega's office were covered with drawings and notes apparently from her young students. Each one was framed as if it were in a museum. It appeared as though she was a huge fan of children's art.

Just as Blake finished a walk around the entire space, Ms. Ortega entered the room.

"Welcome!" she said, extending her hand to shake his. "I'm so glad you came. I've been looking forward to your visit."

"You have?"

"Yes, indeed. Joe called and told me about your time together. He told me that you are an amazing young man."

"I am?"

"Yes, that's what he said. He also said you had only one question—something about leadership character."

"Well, I came here with one question, now I have two."

"What's the new question?" Molly asked.

"What's up with all the children's artwork?"

"Thanks for asking," she began. "These are some of the thank-you notes I've received from my students over the years."

"Some of them? There must be a hundred."

"Yes, over the years, I'm thankful to say I've gotten thousands of them."

"Thousands?"

"Yes. The reason they hang here, and more at my home, is to serve as a constant reminder of why I do what I do. They are the fuel for my engine. They are the reason I lead with all diligence. I really believe the somewhat tired phrase—'children are our future,' and I'm blessed to have the chance to shape that future." She looked at the wall and smiled.

Then, turning to Blake, she said, "Now back to your story. Tell me why," Molly said, motioning for Blake to have a seat.

"Why?" Blake said having missed something in the transition.

"Why do you want to know about leadership character?" Molly said, bringing Blake back to where she had left off a few moments previously.

"Thanks for asking. My answer has actually changed in the past week."

"It has. Why has it changed?"

"My meetings with Chad and Joe changed it."

"And what did they say that had an impact on your thinking?"

"Several things; the biggest was probably something Joe said: 'Without leadership character, no one cares about my skills.'"

"He's right, you know." Molly affirmed Joe's idea.

"Yes, I believe he is, based on what I know about leadership. It makes perfect sense."

"So, my answer to why I wanted to know about leadership character *was* really to get a promotion. Now, with Joe's insight, I want to learn about leadership character to strengthen my overall leadership and get ready for future opportunities."

"Well, the good news is you aren't starting from scratch. Few leaders are. Your parents invested deeply in you, helping you become the man you are today."

"I understand that now. But, I'm thankful it's never too late to strengthen my leadership character."

"Me, too." Molly added.

"So, my visits are intended to help me develop and demonstrate leadership character."

"Good, just what I thought. So, let me ask you directly, Blake, 'How are leaders different?'"

"I'm here to ask you that question," Blake protested slightly.

"I know that's why you're here, but I think you know at least part of the answer. I just want you to know that you know."

"Joe told me leaders need to expect the best."

"That's clearly important." Molly had the same affirming quality he liked so much about his time with Debbie. "What else?"

Blake opened his notebook and began to fidget. "Chad said, the best leaders think others first. Beyond those two ideas, I'm not really sure. I really am trying to figure it out."

"Name one thing you admire about leaders," Molly prodded.

"They get stuff done."

"Fantastic, let's work with that. Why are they able to get stuff done?"

"I'm not sure I've thought much about that," Blake admitted.

"At the risk of oversimplification, I'd like to focus today on one aspect of a leader's character that enables her or him to get things done—"

"What is it?" Blake was delighted he was back to asking the questions.

"Leaders **respond with courage**," Molly said.

Blake added this to his notes.

Facets of Leadership Character

Think Others First

Expect the Best

Respond with Courage

"Why did you choose to say it like that? Couldn't you have just said courage?"

"Sure. But courage doesn't exist in a vacuum. Courage is a response. When faced with a challenging or difficult situation, the best leaders most often respond with courage; less mature leaders, or nonleaders often choose another path—a path with less risk, less conflict, and less personal discomfort."

"What does this look like in your day-to-day world?" Blake asked.

"Much of what I do as a leader is captured in the idea, respond with courage. It is what enables me to 'get stuff done' as you referred to earlier."

"To prevent our teachers and our students from getting behind requires a courageous response. When I see a teacher struggling, I act. I don't wait. When I see a student falling behind, we get on it right away. We try to anticipate as much as we possibly can. And when we see something we don't like beginning to surface, we take action. When I see that we're not hitting our budget numbers, we move to correct the situation. When we see a school in the district not keeping up, we create a plan immediately.

"If you wait, you're often too late and then you've effectively given your leadership away at that point. Leaders usually don't wait—they initiate. This is the courageous response; this is the leadership response."

"It sounds like leaders don't wait. Why not?" Blake asked.

"Well, sometimes leaders do wait. Timing matters. And, sometimes, waiting is the right thing to do. But nonleaders will wait forever.

"So, why the urgency?" Blake asked.

Leaders usually don't wait— they initiate.

"I guess it's probably different for different leaders, but for me, it's because I have a white-hot passion for the cause. The stakes are too high to wait. In my case, we're dealing with the lives of thousands of children."

She paused and looked around the office at the drawings. "The work is too important to be passive about it. The kids give me the courage to act."

"Have you missed it before—waited when you should have acted?"

"Absolutely. If you have an expectation for leaders to be perfect, you need to get in a different game. What I'm talking about today, responding with courage, is a lifelong pursuit. Sometimes I guess wrong, sometimes I'm scared to act, sometimes I'm distracted, and sometimes, I hate to admit it, I'm lazy. Many things can steal our courage.

"Let me tell you about a time a combination of these factors stole my courage. I had received several complaints from parents about a particular teacher. I asked the principal from that school to look into it. I was busy; I was hoping he could turn things around. He didn't. Several children failed because of my lack of courage."

"Wasn't it his fault—the teacher, or even the principal?"

"I've been challenged recently by a friend of mine named Dr. Henry Cloud. He says leaders get what they create and what they allow. The responsibility for those children rests with me. I am the leader, and in this case, I failed to respond with courage. In retrospect, I could have handled that situation very differently. I'll do better in the future. The kids are counting on me."

"Can you give me some other examples of how leaders demonstrate their courage?" Blake asked with pen in hand.

"Leaders respond with courage when they:

Articulate the vision for the future.

Build relationships with challenging people.

Challenge people to grow and change.

Mend broken relationships.

Confront difficult problems.

Make hard or unpopular decisions.

"Leaders respond with courage. It's a critical element of leadership character. Without it, your success as a leader will always be limited."

"How can a person develop the ability to respond with courage?" Blake asked.

"Practice taking action," Molly began. "When you think, I should call so and so, don't wait. Do it then. When you see your new neighbor across the street, don't wait to meet her. Do it now. When you have an idea, look for an appropriate forum to share it, and do it soon. See how many times every day you can take the initiative. When you meet someone for the first time, introduce yourself. Ask the first question to start the conversation. When you encounter a problem, offer a solution. As you go through your day, ask yourself what action would be appropriate here?"

Each action you take, big or small, will require a measure of courage. Most of the time, small amounts; other times, more courage will be required. You'll discover that it's often not as hard as you might have previously thought."

"What happens when a leader fails to respond with courage?" Blake asked.

"Most of the time, the consequences are real but unseen in the moment."

"What do you mean?"

"I'll give you a two-part answer—one from my leadership and one hypothetical example from your world.

"Remember the story I shared about my lack of courage in dealing with a problem teacher. It was months before the consequences were felt. They were real all along but didn't come to fruition until the end of the school year. That's the thing that makes courage so valuable. It is not always obvious that it's even needed. Leaders can develop an instinct to inform them when action is required. It's part experience, part judgment, with a dash of wisdom thrown in for good measure.

"Here's an example from your world—at work, when you're in a meeting wrestling with an important issue and you choose not to share your ideas, what happens?"

"I may miss an opportunity to contribute."

"Correct. Although your voice was absent in the debate and your ideas remained quarantined in your mind, were the consequences obvious? Probably not, but neither were your courage displayed and your ideas valued by your peers and the organization. The consequences of your inaction were not immediate nor obvious.

"When you don't respond in a meeting you may also miss the chance to serve another team member. If you've got a better idea than the one being pursued and you fail to respond with courage, you're hindering the performance of your team and the organization. None of these consequences is felt immediately, but all are still very real.

"Your missed opportunities are often no big deal in isolation. They are, however, cumulative. One seemingly insignificant missed opportunity after another—another chance to add value missed. Over time, you'll not be seen as courageous. You may not be seen as a leader either. Leaders respond with courage.

Your missed opportunities
are often no big deal in isolation.
They are, however, cumulative.

"How about at home, what happens when you miss an opportunity there?" Molly asked.

"I guess—it could hurt my marriage."

"It certainly could. How about with your son?"

"If I don't respond with courage, I may miss an opportunity to help Clint learn and grow. Thanks for helping me personalize this idea. It's big."

"How well do you do this now?" Molly asked.

"I don't think I'm great at this. Occasionally." He paused. "But not consistently. I've been much more focused on just doing what I'm told."

"There's nothing wrong with doing what you're told—leaders have to do that, too," Molly said.

"But, because leaders develop a habit of responding with courage, I'm guessing they have to be told what to do less often," Blake added.

"Absolutely! Think about the word leader—the one in the lead, the one out front, the one who has gone ahead of the others; the one who responds with courage often finds himself in the lead position.

"To respond with courage, and the initiative it demonstrates, is one of the marks of great leaders. Their willingness to respond with courage, time and time again, makes leaders different from followers." Molly said it, as if she were done.

"Thank you for your time today. I'd like to be able to call on you if I have follow-up questions."

"Certainly. I'll be happy to meet with you again."

Blake had mixed emotions after the meeting. Responding with courage was not a strength for him. He would need to work on this. But he was glad the idea was easy to understand: Leaders don't wait, they respond with courage!

The Price of Leadership

Blake was excited to meet with Debbie to update her on his previous visit.

This morning, Blake and Debbie met in the parking lot as they approached the shop.

"How are you this morning?" Debbie asked.

"I'm doing okay."

Debbie knew Blake well enough to know he wasn't telling her the whole truth.

"Okay . . . " she hesitated. "Let's get our drinks and find a table." A few moments later they were seated in their usual spot.

"How'd the meeting go with Molly?"

"Well, Molly clearly lives out her belief that leaders respond with courage."

"She does. That's one of the reasons many people love her . . . and others don't."

"I guessed that responding with courage would not always be popular," Blake said.

"Your instincts are correct, not everyone is a fan of Molly Ortega." Debbie affirmed Blake's intuition. "It just wouldn't be productive to display some of the letters and emails she receives," Debbie said with a grin.

"I guess making everyone happy is out of the question," Blake said, thinking out loud.

"When leaders lead well, not everyone is going to be happy."

"Wouldn't that be a good goal?"

"If you feel the need to make everyone happy, you should be a wedding planner not a leader."

"I don't understand," Blake confessed.

Debbie explained, "Leaders don't try to make people unhappy. However, leaders just know, progress is always preceded by change."

"And some people don't like change," Blake added.

"Right. So if we're leading well, we're driving change. The unfortunate by-product is almost always some unhappy people.

"Let's take Molly as an example. She has always been willing to initiate necessary change. This requires courage. Did she tell you she terminated several principals in the district last year?"

"No, she didn't mention that."

"She also closed two schools and removed more than a dozen teachers. She took action. She didn't wait. As a result, she didn't make everyone happy."

"Wow. We didn't talk about that side of responding with courage." Blake had to process that a minute.

"If there were no challenge, there would be no need for courage—or leadership. It's one of the hardest parts of the job."

"How did she know she was doing the right thing when she closed schools and terminated faculty?"

"You'll have more insight on the answer to that question after a few more visits. How are you doing on responding with courage?"

"Not very well, I'm afraid."

Debbie thought to herself, this must be why he's not himself this morning. "Please tell me more."

"I would say more hit-and-miss. I seem to have lost some of my courage over the years. Is that possible?"

"Sure. It happens all the time. You often see that in people who feel defeated or hopeless."

"I'm not hopeless," Blake protested.

"I'm not saying you are; I'm just saying that is one of the circumstances that suppress courage."

"What else?"

"Fear, stress, workload."

"How can workload diminish courage?"

"If you've got more work than you can physically do, you're less likely to enter the fray and make a courageous decision. However, once you've cultivated any leadership character trait, it usually shows up in one form or another."

"Why?"

"Leadership character, like other character traits, once established, is hard to hide. Someone once defined character as who you are when no one is looking. It's not what you do as much as it is who you are—or are becoming. So, with this definition, you can see that it is not really possible to turn it off. If you're breathing, you are living out who you are."

"You've given me a lot to think about," said Blake, reflecting on what he had just heard.

Leadership character, like other character traits, once established, is hard to hide.

"What are your action items thus far?" Debbie continued.

"I am going to look for ways to respond with courage and put those new muscles to work—hopefully, every day."

"Send me an email at the end of the week and let me know how it's going."

. . .

Back at work, Blake was looking for ways to respond with courage. He didn't want to do anything crazy. He did notice the building needed painting but decided not to say anything about that.

He felt as though he was looking at his role through different lenses now. However, his vision had not yet adjusted to the new prescription.

While looking at the financials for his team, Blake noticed a disturbing pattern. One of his clients was chronically late on payments. Was this an opportunity to respond with courage? He wasn't sure. He decided to talk to Samantha and stopped by her office that afternoon.

"Samantha, have you got a minute?"

"Sure, what's up?"

"I was looking at our accounts receivables this morning and noticed that Lambert Systems seems to have developed a pattern of late payments. Has anybody looked into that?"

"No, I don't think so. They ultimately pay us, and they're a long-term client."

"I understand that. It just seems like having several million dollars consistently late matters."

"You're right. What do you propose?"

"Let me go see them. I think we've got a good relationship."

"I'm not sure. We really don't want to tick them off. We need their business."

"I know. Can I talk with them?"

"Okay, but be careful. If you blow this, I'm not sure I can cover for you."

"Believe me, I'll be careful."

As Blake left Samantha's office, he had a new appreciation for responding with courage. He was scared!

He scheduled a meeting with Greg Lambert, the owner of the company. Greg's father had started the business, and Greg had been running the place for about two years. Interestingly enough, that's when the slow payments had started.

When Blake scheduled the meeting, he asked for just fifteen minutes with Mr. Lambert. He was pleased that the appointment was scheduled so quickly.

On the day of the meeting, Blake arrived early and sat in the lobby rehearsing what he planned to say.

When he finally saw Mr. Lambert, the conversation was much easier than he thought. He introduced himself and asked if Greg was satisfied with the products and services that Dynastar was providing. Blake was thankful he said yes.

"Well, Mr. Lambert, we love having you as a client, and we've enjoyed this relationship since your father started your company. I'm here to ask for your help."

"Sure, what do you need?"

"I've noticed a pattern in your payments over the past few years."

"Is there a problem?"

"Well, sir . . . we do get paid."

"And?"

"And the payments are typically sixty to ninety days late."

"They are?" Mr. Lambert sounded puzzled.

"Yes, sir."

"That's not the way we do business."

"Can you please have someone on your team take a look? We truly enjoy serving you and your company. And, the truth is, our company would be stronger if your payments were more timely.

"I won't look into it."

Blake's heart stopped.

"I'll fix it."

Blake breathed a sigh of relief.

"Blake, thank you for bringing this to my attention. I'm guessing there's a systems problem somewhere. If I find out anything different, I'll let you know. Consider the problem solved."

"Thank you, sir. Please call on me, or any member of our team, if we can serve you in the future."

"Again, thank you, Blake."

Back at the office, Blake reported to Samantha. "We'll wait and see," Blake said. "I believe he's going to get this straightened out."

"Thank you, Blake, that was a good call on your part. Gutsy and also the right thing to do."

"I'm glad I could help."

. . .

At home, Blake told Megan some of what he had learned from his visits. He also told her about his visit with Mr. Lambert.

"It all makes sense to me," Megan said as she wiped the peas off Clint's arms. "What you're saying is what I've seen the best leaders do."

The conversation with Megan reminded him that Megan had been an emerging leader in her firm before they decided to have a family.

"Does it all make sense to you?" she asked as Clint grabbed the butter off the table.

"It makes sense; I'm just trying to figure out what to do with it."

"Be yourself."

"Being myself hasn't gotten me a promotion."

"I know enough about leadership to know two things," Megan said. "One, you don't need a promotion to lead."

"Yes, that's what Debbie says, too."

"Second, you'll lead best out of your strengths. That's what I mean when I say be who you are. Here's something to think about. What are you excited about at work right now?"

"We're bringing in ten new employees next month. They're going to help us all with the current workload."

"Who's going to train them?"

"I guess we'll use the buddy system as we always have. I sure did learn a lot a few years ago from Sam."

"Ten new employees," Megan said. Blake's mind began to race.

Megan continued, "Sounds like an opportunity to me."

"I've got it. I could volunteer to be a training buddy."

"Yes, and?" Megan prompted Blake to finish his thought.

"And I could share with them what I learned working with Sam that could help them maximize their training experience."

"Sure. You love to help people grow. All you need is a little courage to get involved."

Blake leaned across the table and gave Megan a big kiss. "I love you. Thanks for not getting frustrated with me."

"Who said I'm not going to get frustrated with you?" She grinned as she pulled Clint from his high chair. "I'll be frustrated if you don't give Clint a bath."

"I'm on it!"

No Substitute for Wisdom

Blake had learned a great deal from Chad, Joe, and Molly.
He was excited about his next visit too. Victoria Barnett
had been a very successful lawyer and the managing partner in a large international law firm, before deciding to
stay closer to home and become a judge.

Blake arrived early at the courthouse for his meeting
with Judge Barnett. As he approached her office, he saw
about a dozen young people leaving. They appeared to be
about his age, maybe a little younger. As he introduced
himself to the judge's assistant, he asked about the group.

"Law students," she said. "The judge meets with a
group like that every week. She helps them make sense of
what they're learning. She loves to help young people."

"That's why I'm here."

"You said you were referred by Debbie Brewster?"

"Yes, do you know her?"

"I do, she's a fine lady. She's helped her share of young
people over the years." She took Blake into a large room.
It was a library and conference area with a large table.

"Good morning! You're starting your day early," the judge said.

"Not as early as those students who just left," Blake said.

"Well, one way I determine who is serious and who's not is by setting a rigorous schedule. When your weekly session begins at 6:00 AM, some self-select out." She smiled warmly.

"I've been looking forward to our visit," the judge added. "Debbie always introduces me to amazing young people, men and women like you."

"Hold your praise until after we've talked." Blake smiled, and added, "Amazing is a high bar . . . I'm just a guy with a question."

"What's your question?"

"How do you recognize and develop leadership character?" Blake asked.

"Anything else?"

"Well, after you answer that question, I'd like the chance to offer a few follow-up questions."

"Fair enough," the judge said. "But before I answer your question, tell me why you want to know."

By this point on his journey, Blake had revised his response to this important question. He summarized it as follows: "I want to strengthen my leadership character so I can serve more effectively at home and at the office. I want to identify any gaps and work to close them."

"I'm delighted you're here, and applaud your efforts. I'm assuming that someone has told you how difficult the process of character formation can be."

"Yes, ma'am. But I've also been told it is possible."

"It is. That's one reason I meet with young people like the students you saw leaving my office. I'm trying to help them learn about leadership character, too. If young leaders can understand its importance early in their careers, it can make a huge difference in the opportunities that await them and the impact they have on others."

The judge continued, "I'm assuming you've made multiple visits on your journey thus far?"

"Yes, I have."

"Outstanding—here's my contribution to the conversation about leadership character: The best leaders **hunger for wisdom**."

"That's interesting," he said.

"Why do you think the best leaders want wisdom?" Victoria asked.

"I don't know. I've never really thought about it. Maybe they're trying to prove something?"

"For some leaders, that might be their motivation. But if you embrace a think others first mindset, I'm assuming Chad talked to you about that?"

"Yes, he did," Blake confirmed.

"Then, you hunger for wisdom so you can better serve those entrusted to your leadership."

Blake was delighted to add this next piece of the puzzle.

Facets of Leadership Character

Think Others First

Expect the Best

Respond with Courage

Hunger for Wisdom

"I need you to say a little more about how wisdom helps leaders serve."

"Leadership done well is very difficult. Wisdom is essential. It informs our decisions, and ultimately, leaders succeed or fail based on their decisions."

"Which decisions are critical?"

"All of them—people decisions, strategy decisions, financial decisions, how you invest your time, and on and on. The list of decisions that define a leader is very long. Wisdom is needed to make every one of those decisions."

"So, are we really talking about decision-making?"

"Here's how I think about it: Decision-making is a skill. Wisdom is a leadership character trait; wisdom informs our decisions. They're different, but there is clearly a synergistic relationship."

"What if we don't have the wisdom gene?"

"I believe wisdom can and must be forged over time," Victoria added.

"Forged," Blake said. "I'm guessing you chose that word deliberately."

"I did. When metal is forged, it is a difficult process. There is heat, smoke, fire, friction, time, and usually a guy with a hammer." She smiled.

"It may be difficult for the blacksmith—but it's painful for the metal," Blake added.

"And the same can be said for forging this element of leadership character," she added.

"How do you cultivate this hunger for wisdom?"

"As with many things in life, there is no exact formula. How do you love? How do you create? How do you live a life with no regrets? However, I have a few practices to suggest that may prove helpful."

"I'm ready," Blake said.

"Focus on the pursuit not the outcome," the judge said.

"I'm guessing that's why you chose the word 'hunger,'" Blake added.

"Yes, you need to think of your quest for wisdom as a hunger that will never be satiated. The mere thought that you've arrived will spawn pride and arrogance."

"Okay, what else can I do?"

"Be open to input, new ideas, contrarian opinions, and views. Be open to the truth that you and I know very little about the world. Even in our area of expertise, we must admit that our knowledge of the topic pales against all that is knowable.

A commitment to lifelong learning will help you maintain this openness. The pursuit of wisdom requires an open mind, and an open mind can be fueled by learning. Leaders who desire wisdom must become predatory in their search for wisdom."

You need to think of your quest for wisdom as a hunger that will never be satiated.

"What does that look like to a twenty-something, entry-level employee?"

"You need to be constantly growing."

Blake was having a flashback to his time with Debbie five years before. "Debbie and I have talked about that a lot over the years."

"Great! She and I have spent hours discussing the same subject. Just continue to be intentional about learning. If you persist, you'll be a better, wiser leader; I promise."

"I'm already working on this. I have been since I started at Dynastar. Anything else?"

"One last idea for today: Establish a network of counselors to call on for their advice and wisdom. I'm guessing you and Debbie talked about this; that's really what your visits are all about."

"Who do you get counsel from?" Blake asked.

"I get counsel from my husband, my closest friends, other judges, lawyers I respect, my assistant—"

"Hold on, you get counsel from your assistant?"

"Yes, she gives some of the best counsel of all. Why does that surprise you?"

"I don't know, it just sounds strange to me."

"Let's go back to my previous suggestion; you've got to be open," Victoria reminded Blake.

She continued. "Who knows you better in a work setting than your assistant? She knows your strengths, your weaknesses, your struggles, and she understands how you make a unique contribution to the organization. I certainly want this person to provide counsel for me. Over the years, my best performance reviews have come from my assistants."

"Seriously—your assistant gives you a performance review?"

"Yes—I guess you met Kristie when you arrived today. She's been an amazing counselor for me over the years. She's been willing to tell me the truth—the whole truth—even when I really didn't want to hear it. It has been a tremendous gift. I'm where I am today, in large part, due to the counsel of others. I've borrowed their wisdom."

"You've certainly stretched my thinking," Blake said.

"A hunger for wisdom fueled by a commitment to lifelong learning will equip you for whatever lies ahead."

"Amazing! That's why a hunger for wisdom must be part of a leader's character." Blake continued, thinking out loud, "I've got a lot to think about here. I do want to hunger for wisdom. I just need to be more intentional."

"You're starting from a good place," Victoria offered reassuringly.

"I am?"

"Yes, I know enough about your life to know the ideas we're discussing are already part of your leadership character."

"They are?"

"Sure. You met Debbie years ago; she's been mentoring you. I'd say our time today and the other visits you'll make are another example. I could easily be convinced that you're demonstrating a hunger for wisdom."

"Thanks for your confidence. It feels like I just let my hunger for wisdom fall off my radar for a while."

"It seems like you're back on course. With a decided heart and discipline, you can constantly strengthen your leadership character. Leaders know this, pursue it, and celebrate it."

"Thank you for your help!"

Please call on me if you want to meet again, and you're always welcome as a guest in my 6:00 AM mentoring sessions."

"I may take you up on that. Thanks again."

As Blake left the judge's office, he couldn't help thinking about his life and career up until now. Despite the nice things Victoria had said, he had taken his eye off the ball; he was not focused on learning. Before his next interview, he wanted to meet with Debbie again. He was thankful they had now established a regular monthly meeting, and he would see her in a few days.

. . .

Blake arrived earlier than usual to think about what he'd learned so far. He was on his second cup of coffee when Debbie arrived.

"You must have gotten here early," Debbie said, looking at the number of discarded sugar packets on the table. "How are you?"

"Well," Blake began. "I'm learning a lot on my visits. Thanks for setting me up to meet with these amazing leaders."

"My pleasure."

"I've learned that I'm not the only one you've sent on this scavenger hunt."

"You are correct. Does that matter?"

"Not really. I was just curious, how did those visits turn out?"

"What do you mean by 'turn out?'"

"Did everyone you sent get it?"

"If you mean, did they learn the specific traits of leadership character, yes, they all got it."

"That's probably not my real question. Were they all able to embrace what they learned and become a better leader?"

"No, unfortunately not," she said in a tone that reflected some sadness.

"Why not?" Blake was already concerned; this conversation wasn't making him feel any better.

"Three reasons, I think."

"Some of the people I've tried to help never got past the 'leadership is a title' dilemma. That became their Achilles' heel. They were so preoccupied with their position, or lack of a position, in the organization, they were blinded to the daily opportunities to lead. As you and I have discussed before, a title doesn't make someone a leader—and the absence of a title shouldn't keep someone from leading."

"That makes sense in my head, but for some reason, I still stumble on this one myself," Blake admitted.

"I think that's a tremendous insight. Because you recognize this tendency in yourself, you've got a better chance of beating it. 'I have a problem' is the first step toward a cure."

"I look forward to being cured," Blake chuckled as he thought about his problem. "What's the second reason?"

"Fear is probably the second thing that held some of them back. Fear has stolen the future of countless leaders."

"Fear of what?" Blake was taking copious notes.

"A fear of failure, fear of the unknown, and even a fear of the responsibility that comes with leadership."

"Leadership can be scary; even I know that from my high school football days. There is a lot of pressure."

"Yes, and some men and women, even some already in positions of leadership, give in to the fear."

"I hope that won't be me."

"It will. At some point or another, the fear gets all of us. We've just got to work to see that it doesn't happen too often."

As he heard her comment, Blake reflected on how much he admired Debbie for telling the truth. He wasn't sure how she always did it in such an encouraging fashion. All he knew was that he needed to hear the truth. He was thankful she cared enough to tell him.

"That's a sobering thought" was all Blake answered.

"Leadership is a privilege, but it is not free—it comes at a price."

"Thanks for reminding me. What's the third reason?" Blake asked.

"And finally—" Debbie stopped. "I'll hold this one. Because one of the things you've yet to learn is the biggest stumbling block of all. We'll talk about the third reason later."

"Don't leave me hanging here," Blake was impatient.

"All I'll say is this: It's a matter of the heart."

"What do I do with that?"

"Nothing at the moment," she smiled. "You've got one visit left?"

"Yes, I'm scheduled to meet with Coach Tom Bradley."

"Do you know much about him?"

"A little. I know he's an outstanding coach. His team beat our team every year—except one." Blake smiled a big smile.

Leadership is a privilege, but it is not free— it comes at a price.

"I know what you're thinking. You played against his team in the state playoffs."

"Yes, we did."

"And you won. "

"We did."

"What do you remember about that game?"

"I remember every play."

"Yes, I seem to recall you had a big night. Did you know I was at the game?"

"No way! Why were you there?"

"Your dad invited several of us from the office. It was a great night for you and your family. We all wanted to be there to celebrate with your dad—win or lose. Do you remember any other specifics about the night—beyond the individual plays you called?"

"Funny you mention it; I do. I remember the post-game press conference. What Coach Bradley said seemed strange to me at the time."

"What did he say?"

"He said his team was good enough to have won and that the loss was his fault. He said he hoped to use the experience to become a better coach."

"Hold that thought. Go and visit the coach. Talk to him about what he said that night. I think it will help you connect the dots and give you the last piece of the puzzle."

Look in the Mirror

Once again, Blake had attempted to schedule an early meeting. However, with the coach it was more difficult. He already had weight training with his athletes scheduled for 7:00 each morning. So, Blake agreed to meet the coach after practice. He promised Megan he'd bring dinner home after the meeting, which was always a good idea from her perspective.

"Coach, thanks for meeting with me."

"It's great to see you again. And, under more friendly circumstances," he said with a broad smile.

"Oh, you remember me?" Blake had specifically not mentioned their past connection when he scheduled the appointment.

"Yes, I do. You were a fine quarterback. Congratulations on that championship."

"Thank you, sir, and thank you for meeting with me. As I mentioned on the phone, I've been meeting with members of my dad's small group." As Blake said those words, all of a sudden, he had a new question. "Why didn't I know you were meeting with my dad?"

"Maybe because I only had the chance to be in one meeting with him."

"Why just one?"

"It was after the championship game; that's when I met your dad. He introduced himself to me after the press conference and said he wanted me to consider joining a group he was part of.

"I was suspicious. I knew he was a businessman. He told me that it was a group from all walks of life dedicated to being better leaders. He said, 'The world needs more and better leaders—regardless of our individual professions.'

"I thanked him for his offer, but I didn't join the group right away. I waited a few years. Then after I had a really bad season, I knew I had to get better as a leader, and I called your dad. He was still willing to have me in the group. I was so thankful, and still am. But shortly after my first meeting, your dad died. I was very sorry about that for you, your family, and for me, too. I know I could have learned a lot from him."

"I'm sorry, too." Blake said.

"But I can say this, that group is one of the best things I've ever done. They provide encouragement, accountability, learning, and community—as a result, my leadership has improved along the way."

"Do you still meet with them?"

"Yes, we meet twice a month."

"Well, thanks for meeting with me today," Blake said. "As I said on the phone, I have only one question and probably a few follow-up questions."

"Yes, you didn't say who suggested this, but I'm guessing it was Debbie."

"You're right."

"I've talked to other young leaders at her request in the past."

"I guessed that; there's a pattern emerging."

"So, what's your question?"

"What can you tell me about leadership character?" Blake was sure the coach already knew the question before he asked it.

"Who have you met with so far?"

"Chad Culpepper, Mr. Conrad, Ms. Ortega, and Judge Barnett."

"So, I'm the last one?"

"Yes, and I'm excited to hear what you have to say," Blake added.

One thing you've discovered for sure, leadership character is multifaceted; there are several ways leaders are different. Today, I want to share one that is at the core of what it means to be a leader."

Blake seemed to recall something similar from his previous visits; all he could assume is that there are several things at the core of being a leader.

"**Leaders accept responsibility**," the coach said. "It's about ownership."

"Ownership?" Blake didn't even write it down immediately. He wasn't sure what it meant. "What do you mean by ownership?"

"Ownership in this context is about a leader's willingness to assume responsibility for his or her actions and the actions of those they lead. It is about being accountable for actions and outcomes—yours and others."

That made some sense to Blake, but he had never considered ownership a character trait of great leaders. Before he began his follow-up questions, he added it to his notes:

Facets of
Leadership Character

Think Others First

Expect the Best

Respond with Courage

Hunger for Wisdom

Accept Responsibility

"Don't all leaders have this trait?" Blake wondered out loud.

"No, unfortunately, many do not. But the great ones all have it. They are willing to assume responsibility for the vision and their progress toward it. They are willing to accept ultimate responsibility when the team fails. They are very slow to blame others. If something happens on their watch, it's their accountability."

"It sounds intense to me."

"Intense?" Coach said, "in what way?"

"Intense, heavy—like a burden. Something a leader has to carry for the entire team or organization."

"There is no doubt it has weight, but the best leaders carry it gladly."

"Why are leaders willing to do it—carry it, I mean?"

"Some leaders accept responsibility because they are 'responsible' people. This is not a bad thing. However, what the best leaders have at their core is a different sense of responsibility. It's not because someone delegated something to them; it's because they believe deeply in the vision and purpose of the cause.

"This type of responsibility is an extremely powerful force. So powerful, men and women will not only accept responsibility for their own actions, they willingly accept it for those they lead."

"Coach, I saw you do this—accept responsibility," Blake interrupted. "I wasn't sure I wanted to bring this up, but after the state championship game . . . " His voice trailed off.

"Yes, I remember."

"Was it hard for you to accept responsibility the way you did?"

"Not really, losing a game is never fun, but it's all part of the journey."

"So, translate it for me. Why wasn't it hard to accept responsibility for the game?"

"To blame others is not the path leaders take. Leaders accept responsibility, in part, because they are sold out to the vision. It matters more than they do."

"What's your vision?" Blake asked.

"To help young men become champions for life, on and off the field."

"That's big."

"The most compelling visions usually are," the coach admitted.

The best leaders don't blame others. They own their actions and their outcomes.

"So back to the championship—if my young men are going to be champions off the field, they need to see their leaders accept responsibility. To blame others—the officials, the coaching staff, my players, the opponents, even the playing conditions—" He paused and smiled.

"Yeah, I'll never forget that night. I've never been that cold and wet since then." Blake shivered at the memory.

The coach finished his thought, "The best leaders don't blame others. They own their actions and their outcomes."

Blake wanted to summarize what he'd just heard.

"So, when the team lost, your team lost, and you, as their leader, you had to own it."

"Yes. I wanted to own it. It was my responsibility."

"Let's assume a leader doesn't have this desire or ability to accept responsibility; what can that leader do?"

"That's a formidable challenge. We're really talking about the way someone sees the world. But I do think there are some things leaders can do to strengthen their willingness to accept responsibility."

"Fantastic! I need some help thinking about this," Blake confessed.

"Pretend you own the outcome," the coach said.

"Pretend I own the outcome for what?" Blake asked.

"Everything you work on—even if you are not the project lead . . . or the quarterback."

"That's a new thought."

Coach Bradley continued, "As I understand this, some people have a real advantage here. Psychologists have found that some people believe this without much effort. Others find it virtually impossible to assume responsibility for outcomes. The clinical term for this is locus of control. Here's the core question: Do you believe your actions affect outcomes or not? If you say yes, you have an internal locus of control—you believe you have at least some control. If you say no, believing you have little or no control over outcomes, you have an external locus of control."

"Give me another example. This is something I must have slept through in psych class."

"When something happens at work that you were clearly involved in and it doesn't turn out quite right, what's your first reaction? To blame others, circumstances, or events? Or to accept responsibility?"

"I probably run and hide. What does that mean?" Blake managed a very forced smile.

"It means you've probably got some work to do here."

"Can you give me one more example?

"Okay, I've been told that if you survey men and women in prison, most of them will say it was someone else's fault they're in jail. They would blame the judge, the jury, their partner, their lawyer, their mother, or the system. Very few of them would say, 'I own my circumstances; I made a mistake; I made a bad decision.'"

"This sounds like something I should work on right away or my life and career could end badly."

"Yes, if you and I as leaders pretend we own the outcomes, it will:

Change our level of engagement
Increase our level of buy-in
Change the way we see people and the work

Before you know it, we'll change, and we really will feel like we own the outcomes. Then it will be very natural for us to accept responsibility."

"Here's another way to think about it: Every time you experience an outcome that doesn't meet your expectations, look in the mirror and ask yourself how you contributed to that failure. Ask yourself what you'll need to do differently in the future to get a different result. Identify lessons from every failure—personal, team, or organizational. A great question to ask is, 'What did I do, or fail to do, that contributed to this outcome?'"

"What did you learn from our big game?" Blake asked.

"Several things, as I recall. You mentioned the cold, wet weather."

"Yes, it was a mess."

"Let me ask you a question. Do you remember your practice schedule the week before the game?"

"Not in detail—is there something specific you're looking for?"

"Was it a typical week?"

"Sure."

"And you practiced outside?"

"Yes, sir. Didn't you guys have a typical week?"

"No, I made a bad decision—or two. We didn't have a typical week. I reduced our practice time and because of the cold, wet weather, we practiced in the gym."

"Oh." Blake was shocked, "Why did you do that?"

"I was overconfident, and I wanted my players to like me," Tom said without hesitation.

"Really?"

"Yes, on both counts. Both are traps that snag even veteran leaders from time to time. First, we were good; I knew that, and our team knew that. We were the defending state champs."

"Twice in a row as I recall."

"Yes, we were. I didn't take you guys seriously enough—pride is a dangerous thing.

"Combine this with my need to please people, and you've got a recipe for disaster. My team captain came to me and said, 'Coach, let's practice indoors. What a great gift to the team for a hard season. You'll be their hero.' I still remember how appealing that sounded to me. I let my personal desire to be their hero override my responsibility to be their leader."

"But I'm guessing your coaching staff was part of the decision to change the routine?"

"Yes, but it was my call. I accept responsibility for my decisions. We got to the game, and my players were not ready—they were cold and wet and distracted by their circumstances when we really needed to focus. I accept responsibility for that."

"I remember you said some of that in the postgame press conference."

"Yes, I did. And I apologized to my team that night. I hate it for the boys. Who knows?" He smiled. "If I had been a better leader, we might have given you a better game."

"It sounds like looking in the mirror is something you do a lot."

"More than you might imagine. It changes your heart and your actions. But, there's one more thing for you to consider. You don't want to accept all the responsibility."

"I thought that was the point."

"Not exactly. When things do go well you don't need to accept responsibility, you want to give praise.

"The best leaders understand their role is to help others win. If I, as the leader, take all the responsibility, including the praise, do you think those I lead feel like they've won?"

"No, I guess not."

"Let's think back to your coach's comments after the game. What if he had stood up and said, 'I did a great job preparing the team. I did an amazing job calling the plays. This is the greatest victory of my career.' How would you and the team have felt?"

"It wouldn't have felt the same—that's for sure. I think we'd be less likely to follow his leadership the next year."

"Exactly, I didn't hear your coach's remarks after the game, but I'm guessing he gave you and the team ample praise for your hard work and your accomplishments. Am I correct?"

"Yes, you're right." Blake was immediately distracted as he thought back to *his* postgame press conference. He was mortified. As he recalled, all he talked about was how well *he* played. No mention of the linemen, the running backs, the defense or the coaching staff. It was all about him. As Blake thought back on that night, he began to lose the color in his face; he felt like he was going to be sick.

The coach could sense something was up. "Blake, are you okay?"

Regaining a bit of composure, Blake said, "Sure, I'm so thankful my dad invited you to join his group all those years ago. I'm also thankful I've had the chance to reconnect with you. Thanks for your counsel. I'm going to do a much better job of accepting responsibility going forward."

When Blake got to his car, he sat there and stared out the window for a very long time. He knew he'd just discovered the biggest gap in his leadership character.

He thought, I tend to blame others when things don't go my way. And, to make matters worse, when things go well, I take all the credit. What a slime ball! Why hasn't anyone ever brought this up before? He was angry—not with anyone in particular—just angry. Then it hit him. He was doing it again! He was blaming unknown people who could or should have told him. Well, now he'd been told. This is in my control. I can do better, he thought. I can change this.

I Can Change This

Blake left the meeting with the coach with a new spirit. He knew that he didn't control his future but no longer felt like a victim. His outlook was different—his actions were within his control. Blake's confidence in himself and his future had risen. Not that anything he'd learned would be a revelation to Debbie, but he wanted to share his insight with her. Their next meeting was still a few weeks away but Blake decided to call her anyway. He picked up the phone.

"Hi, Debbie, I just had a fantastic meeting with Coach Bradley. I'd love to tell you about it. I know we've got a meeting scheduled; any chance we can meet sooner?"

Blake was glad Debbie was available to meet the next morning. After he hung up the phone, he remembered that he was supposed to buy dinner for the family. He stopped by Megan's favorite Chinese restaurant on the way home. He called to let her know he was on the way.

"I'll be home soon. I can't wait to share what I learned from the coach this afternoon. I love you!"

As she hung up the phone, Megan could sense something about Blake had changed. It was nothing he said, just the way he said it. Her instincts were correct. Blake had assumed personal responsibility for the process of strengthening his leadership character.

When he arrived home, he gave Megan a huge hug and said, "I'm sorry."

"Sorry for what?" Megan said.

"I've been missing something for many, many years."

"What's that?"

"I've been blaming others."

"For what?"

"For everything. Everything, except the good things. I've been totally comfortable with accepting credit for those things."

"I don't think I understand," Megan confessed.

"I'll explain over dinner. I'm starved."

Over the next forty-five minutes, Blake and Megan had a wonderful conversation, a combination confessional and therapy session.

"That's a lot to process," Megan said.

"I know. But in the past few hours, I've seen my life through a new lens. I've had flashbacks of hundreds of situations in which I failed to accept responsibility. It's no wonder people don't see my leadership potential. I've not demonstrated leadership character."

"That sounds rather definitive," Megan challenged.

"Yeah, and the truth is I've got other things to work on as well. But, I'm convinced this is the big hurdle for me."

"Why do you think it's been hard for you to accept responsibility?"

"I don't know. I'm going to see if Debbie can help me with this one when we meet tomorrow. But the good news is that I can change this. I can do better. Please forgive me for all the times I blamed you for things over the years. Even though I didn't always say that something was your fault, I'm guessing you could tell when that's what I was thinking."

"You're right. I can always tell. I forgive you. Can you forgive me?"

"For what?" he said.

"For the same thing. You're not the only one who's ever misplaced blame." She smiled. "Forget your leadership at work for a minute. I think our marriage will be stronger if we get this one right. Let's agree we're going to accept responsibility here at home."

"Agreed. I'll need your help."

"Me, too."

At that moment, Clint let it be known, in a high-pitched yell, that he also needed help. Rather than waiting to see who would get up as they were accustomed to doing, both Blake and Megan jumped up.

"I've got this," she said.

"Me, too," Blake said. Together, they went to see what Clint needed.

. . .

The next morning, Blake was energized. He wanted to share his insight with Debbie and get her interpretation and suggestions. He was also interested in learning more about why some of the leaders Debbie mentored didn't "get it."

"Good morning." This time Blake had managed to arrive before Debbie. She was only fifteen minutes early, but Blake was five minutes ahead of her.

"I got us a table; now let me get you some tea."

"Thanks, Blake."

When he returned to the table, he started talking before he even sat down. "I know we were scheduled to meet in a few weeks, but I really didn't want to wait."

"I'm glad we could meet today. What's got you so fired up?" She smiled.

I get to decide. I choose my response.
No one does that for me.

"Here's the truth, Debbie; all of my visits were productive, especially Chad's challenge to think others first. But I've got to confess, I was still looking for a big revelation. Now, after my visit with the coach, I see my big issue. I've never been good at accepting responsibility—unless things went smashingly well, then I've been all too eager to accept responsibility. This is the breakthrough I've needed."

"And," Debbie began cautiously, "Why do you think this is good news?"

"Because I get to decide. I choose my response. No one does that for me. I can change this . . . can't I?"

"You and I do choose our responses. I'm assuming Tom gave you some specific things to work on?"

"Yes, he did."

"Great. How can I help?"

"When we last met, you said some of the young people you mentored didn't embrace the message. You said there were three reasons. Some couldn't get past the idea that leading had little to do with a formal position of leadership."

"Yes, for reasons I don't fully understand, some people sincerely believe they cannot lead without a title or position. This barrier is insurmountable for some people."

"The second reason, as I recall, is fear."

"That's correct," Debbie said.

"You never told me the third reason. Will you tell me now?"

"I think you need a few more weeks to fully process everything you've learned so far. Trust me, it will be worth the wait," Debbie said.

Reluctantly, Blake agreed. He left the meeting with the nagging question: I wonder why some leaders don't get it? What is the final hurdle?

A Matter of the Heart

The weeks moved quickly, and Blake could see leadership character in action virtually every day. And to his delight, it wasn't always from the men and women who had positions of leadership. This bolstered his confidence even more—he could do this. And, he did. Nothing monumental, but he was seeing more opportunities and taking them. He was developing and demonstrating leadership character, and people were noticing.

One such occasion was Blake's very next team meeting, called to discuss their performance. The numbers looked good in the aggregate. But underneath, there were signs of trouble.

Samantha said, "Overall, I'm pleased. We're not leading the pack, but we're not last."

Rachael chimed in, "We're actually up for the quarter and the year."

"Yes, that's true, but our increases are decreasing," Samantha added.

"Samantha, do you see a problem, or is that just the overall business cycle?" Kim asked.

"The business cycle may be contributing, but there's another problem," Blake said.

"What's the other problem?" Chuck asked.

"Me," Blake said.

Everyone in the room was stunned.

"Excuse me?" Chuck said.

"Yes, if you look at my clients, their orders have been getting smaller over time."

"Why is that?" Samantha asked.

"I don't know. The truth is, I just realized it sitting here this morning. I own it, and I'm on it. I'll give the team a full report at our next meeting. Any thoughts you may have between now and then would be appreciated."

"Thanks, Blake," Samantha said. She looked a little shocked.

The meeting was adjourned, and she stopped Blake in the hall. "Blake, thanks for owning that issue."

"Now, I just need to get it fixed."

"Blake, do you realize you've never done that before."

"Done what?"

"Owned anything."

Blake was hurt by the raw truth in Samantha's statement. "I'm sorry, Samantha. I didn't realize it was that bad. But I own that, too. I'm going to do better."

"Thank you, Blake. Whatever you're doing is working. Keep it up!"

. . .

It was time for Blake's next meeting with Debbie. He was as excited as ever to be meeting with her, but he was not sure what she was going to tell him. He knew there was still one major hurdle out there that tripped up a lot of leaders, and he wasn't sure what it involved.

Rather than meet at their usual place, Blake suggested they meet at Heaven's Kitchen. Debbie agreed.

When he arrived, the place was already open. He walked in and stopped in his tracks. Standing where he'd first seen Chad stood Debbie. And yes, she was giving handshakes and hugs. As Blake stood there staring, someone tapped him on the shoulder.

It was Chad. "Good morning, Blake. Thanks for coming."

"Well, Debbie and I needed a place to meet and this seemed like a good idea. It looks to me like she's been here before."

"Yes, your father introduced his entire group to this place years ago. All of them are regular volunteers. Our guests love them. Let me go relieve Debbie so she can meet with you. It may not be a great place to meet—she's a real celebrity around here. But let's hope you can do your business with minimal interruptions."

Blake wasn't exactly sure what Chad meant by minimal interruptions. He was soon to find out. Debbie came over and sat across from Blake. "Good morning," she said.

"Good morning. I didn't know you knew about this place."

"Yes, your dad introduced it to our group years ago."

"Our group?" Blake said, in a tone that reflected an insight. "Were you in Dad's group, too?"

"Yes, but not at first. I thought you knew that."

"No, I didn't."

"As I think I've told you, early in my career, I was about to lose my job. I was a horrible leader. In desperation, I applied for a new mentoring program at the company. I'm not sure if it was luck, fate, or divine intervention, but I was assigned your father as my mentor. He was the president of the company at the time, and I was just a team leader—the lowest-performing team in the company."

Just then an elderly woman approached the table. "Debbie, I just wanted say hello and thank you for my new coat. It's the warmest one I've ever had." She leaned over to give Debbie a hug. "I love you," she said. Debbie responded, "I love you, too."

Blake's world had been rocked again. Debbie could see the look on his face. "That's Margaret. We've been friends for about five years. Now, where were we?"

"You were telling me about meeting my dad."

"Oh, yes, he became my mentor. He taught me the secret of great leaders."

"The top part of the iceberg?" Blake asked.

"Yes: Great leaders SERVE."

"Chad says you're an expert on that. I want to hear that story on another day."

"It would be my pleasure," Debbie smiled.

As Blake was about to ask Debbie to continue, a young woman came to the table. She wasn't much older than Blake. She was holding a small child, about two years old.

"Excuse me, Debbie, but I just wanted to say hello. Thanks for the ride to the doctor last week. Jacob is better—it was just a cold."

"You can never be too careful during flu season," Debbie smiled.

"Thanks again. I love you."

"You, too."

"See you soon."

"I hope so."

As Debbie sat down, Blake asked, "What's her name?"

"Megan."

Blake wasn't sure if Debbie knew that his wife was named Megan or not; however, his heart made an immediate connection. He said, "What's her story?"

"She lost her job. Then she lost her apartment."

"Where's her husband?"

"Jail . . . forever. I just help where I can." Debbie paused, "Sorry for the interruptions."

"That's okay. Chad warned me; he said you were a celebrity around here.

"Where were we?"

"You were telling me about my dad and the iceberg."

"The top of the iceberg—that's what your dad thought I needed at the time. And he was right! The performance of my team improved drastically. I was promoted to the head of leadership development and more problems began to emerge. We did some good work, but something just wasn't right. After spending more time with your dad, he convinced me that leaders were different. He introduced me to the rest of the iceberg—leadership character."

This time someone approached the table and greeted Debbie but addressed his comments to Blake. It was Larry.

"Good morning, Debbie. It's always great to see you—like sunshine on a cloudy day." He then turned to Blake.

"Mr. Brown, thanks for coming back to see us. Most people who come to visit don't ever come back. It's good to see you again." Larry extended his hand, and Blake responded by shaking Larry's hand and then he stood and gave Larry a hug. Larry turned and went to the line to get his breakfast.

"I guess I'm not the only celebrity around here," Debbie smiled.

"Okay," he said." You didn't know leaders were different until my dad told you."

"I had no clue. But, he didn't tell me. "

"He didn't? I'm confused."

"Well, rather than tell me, he sent me out to discover the answer just as I asked you to do."

"Don't tell me, you visited some of the same people I've visited over the last few weeks."

"Yes, I did."

"And what did you conclude?" Blake wanted to know if his outcome was similar to Debbie's.

"Several things. First, leaders are different. They see the world differently and they cultivate different character traits."

"Leadership character," Blake added.

Yes, and the other thing I learned is that I did fairly well on some of them and not as good on others. The truth is, I really struggled."

"Which one was the most challenging for you?"

"Ones, plural. I didn't cultivate these traits easily. I continue to work on developing them."

"But which one was the hardest for you?" Blake was looking for some encouragement. If Debbie could do it, maybe he could, too.

"I've always struggled with think others first."

"Me, too!" Blake was happy to know he wasn't the only one.

"So, I think I was telling you my story—after learning what I could, your dad invited me to join the group so I could continue the journey. I was thrilled to be a part of it."

"Are you still part of it?

"Yes, although I did take a year off while John was ill. But I'm back with them now."

At that moment, three men approached the table. "Hi, Debbie."

"Hi, guys; let me introduce you to my friend Blake. Blake, meet Roy, Bob, and Samuel. Guys, this is Jeff Brown's son."

"We know. Larry told us. That's why we came by. We wanted to pay our respects. We weren't able to go to the formal service. We just wanted to say thanks for continuing your father's legacy. He was a good man."

"Thank you. I agree completely." Each man got a handshake and a hug from Blake.

As they walked away, Blake said to Debbie, "Do you know their stories?"

"I do."

"I thought you would. I'd like to know them, too."

"Do you want to hear them now?"

"No, I'll come back, and let them tell me themselves."

"That would be great," Debbie said. "So, where were we?"

"There was one thing you mentioned at our last two meetings that you still haven't told me."

"That's correct. I didn't tell you what keeps many leaders from 'getting it.'"

"Right. You said some don't reach their full potential because they couldn't get past the idea that leadership is about a title or a position. You also said some are just too fearful to lead well."

"Right, there is an element of the unknown in leadership. Can I be successful? Can I make good decisions? Can I grow? Can I bounce back from adversity? Do I have what it takes? Will people follow me? There are a lot of unknowns. These fears combined with the fear of failure have thwarted many careers."

"Yes, I've got those ideas in my notes, but you said there's a third reason. And, I believe you said it was the most significant obstacle for most leaders."

"I did."

"What is it?"

"Give me a napkin."

"I knew there would be a treasure map!" Blake said with a playful smile.

"You enjoyed the last one so much, I didn't want to disappoint."

He handed her a napkin.

"When you asked the group members about leadership character, you received five answers."

"Yes, I did."

"Read those to me."

As Blake read aloud, Debbie wrote down each one.

"Think others first, expect the best, respond with courage, hunger for wisdom, and accept responsibility.

When Blake finished reading, Debbie stopped writing and slid the napkin across the table. She had rearranged the five statements.

Hunger for Wisdom

Expect the Best

Accept Responsibility

Respond with Courage

Think Others First

"I didn't see that coming."

"I knew what you would learn at each visit, but I never know the sequence."

"Have all the previous aspiring leaders been surprised?"

"Yes—every one."

"So, what's the challenge?"

"Leadership character is a matter of the heart. If you do all the things we've talked about, it still won't matter if your heart doesn't change."

"Chad told me that when we met. But I'm not sure I completely understand the implications."

"Look back at your notes, and tell me some of the activities that were suggested during your visits."

Blake flipped through his notes. "Ms. Ortega suggested that I take action to build my courage. Judge Barnett said if I hunger for wisdom, I should seek counsel from others. And, Coach Bradley recommended I look in the mirror when things don't go well. He challenged me to learn something I can do better or different every time there is failure or disappointment."

The heart of leadership is a matter of the heart.

"Those are outstanding suggestions. And I'm guessing you've got at least a dozen more on your list."

"Probably."

"Blake, here's the truth: If you do all those activities and your heart doesn't change, you won't be the kind of leader you want to be. Leadership is not about what you do nearly as much as it's about who you are becoming— the heart of leadership is a matter of the heart."

"Chad also told me that to think others first is the most important character trait of the leader." Blake reflected this thought out loud.

"It may be. It is critical. Why do you think it is so important?"

"It reflects your heart."

"Exactly. You and I have to answer the question of motive. Are we a serving leader or a self-serving leader?"

"Many leaders never get over the hurdle that it can't be about them, and that's about your heart."

"So how do we change our hearts?"

"Hard to say," Debbie said and shrugged her shoulders. "I'm not sure we can."

"What? After all of these meetings and all of this insight and wisdom . . . if we can't change our hearts—" Blake stopped in midsentence. He was crushed.

"Hold on. I said, 'I'm not *sure* we can.' Remember some leaders make the change and some don't."

"What are you suggesting?"

"Do the right things. Do them consistently, and see what happens. I have faith in you."

"Why do you have faith in me?" Blake was clearly testing Debbie. Was she merely expecting the best, or was her faith in him grounded in reality?

Debbie seemed ready for Blake's question. "When you interviewed each of your new mentors, did each of them ask you why you wanted to strengthen your leadership character?"

Blake thought about his visits and responded, "Several of them did."

"Did your answer to the question change over the course of your visits?"

"It did."

"How did it change? Were you just more practiced, or did the substance of your response change?" Debbie didn't know the answer to her question, but she was playing a hunch that the journey itself was having an effect on Blake.

"When I started, I was just trying to get a promotion and make my house payment. By my last visit, I had a different objective."

"What was it?"

"I said I wanted to serve more effectively at home and at work."

"It sounds to me like more than your answer has changed." Debbie smiled. "So has your heart."

As Blake sat there reflecting on her comments, Debbie broke the silence. "Let's give out some handshakes and hugs before we leave here today. What do you say?"

"Let's do it!"

The Next Step

As the weeks turned to months, Blake continued doing the things his new mentors had suggested. When his next review rolled around, he was confident. He knew he had miles to go, but he was convinced he was making progress.

The morning of the review, he showed up early and eagerly awaited Samantha's arrival.

"Good morning, Blake. I've been looking forward to our time."

"I have been, as well," Blake said.

Over the next few minutes, Samantha asked Blake to share his perspective on his performance. Blake was candid and complete in his analysis.

"That's a great summary. I agree with your observations. What are you learning?"

"I'm learning a lot. Specifically, I'm learning that I've been focused on just part of my leadership development."

"Can you explain?"

Blake took Samantha's question as a chance to draw the iceberg for her. She was fascinated. She had never seen leadership depicted like that.

"So, I'm so grateful you challenged me during my last review. You were right. Leaders are different. That was a new idea for me. Since then, I've learned, as much as ninety percent of my success as a leader will be determined by my leadership character. I would never have started my search without your feedback. Thanks again!"

"That means a lot to me. I never felt great about my 'coaching' on this issue. I knew I was onto something, but I didn't know how to talk about it. What are you learning about leadership character?"

"I've learned so much. Here are my three biggest takeaways thus far. One, without leadership character, no one cares about your skills.

"Second, there are five core traits that together constitute leadership character. They represent the HEART of leadership:

Hunger for Wisdom

Expect the Best

Accept Responsibility

Respond with Courage

Think Others First

"And third, and thankfully, leadership character can be formed and transformed."

Blake went on to share with Samantha some of the things he was doing to change his heart. He told her he had accepted the challenge and the responsibility to continue growing his skills and strengthen his leadership character.

When they finished reviewing the list, Samantha asked Blake a pointed question, "Why are you doing all of this?"

"I'm doing these things in hopes that my heart will change. I realize that unless my heart changes, my impact on the world will be limited. I really do want to be a servant leader."

"Blake, thank you. Thanks for all you do to serve our clients, our team, and me. I can tell you, your heart is changing. And I'm not the only one who's noticed. Keep doing what you're doing. Regarding what you're learning, will you share this with the team at our next meeting?"

"I would be delighted to."

. . .

Blake left the meeting with a thankful heart. He could hardly wait to share Samantha's perspective with Debbie. He was eagerly anticipating their next meeting. They had agreed not to try to meet at the Kitchen anymore—too many friends there. So, they were back to the old standby, the coffee shop.

They met at 7:00 on the agreed-on morning. They weren't sure why they always said 7:00, because as was their custom, they both arrived at 6:45.

"Good morning!" Debbie said. "How are you?"

"Fantastic, and you?"

"Life is really good. What's next for you, Blake?"

"I'm not sure exactly. I am continuing to work on my heart."

"Every day," Debbie affirmed. "Me, too! I have a big ask for you today."

"Really, what's that?"

"We've decided to add another member to our group. Would you be interested?"

"Are you asking me to fill my dad's seat?"

"No, we're asking Blake Brown, one of the finest emerging servant leaders we've ever met, to join our group."

"Let me talk with Megan. I know you meet two nights a month."

"Yes, we do. And we'd be honored if you'd join us."

"Thanks for the opportunity!"

Epilogue

As Blake continued to forge a new heart, other things in his life changed as well . . .

Things at work got better—a lot better. Blake was asked to lead a new team. It was a lateral move, but it was important work. It gave Blake an even better opportunity to serve the organization and the people on his team. The biggest change, however, was not the work; the biggest change was in Blake.

Although work was still an important part of Blake's life, life was much more fulfilling for him at home. He was becoming his old self—the one that Megan had fallen in love with years before. He and Megan were once again doing life together.

Blake discovered a passion to serve the homeless. In addition to volunteering at Heaven's Kitchen, he was asked to serve on Chad's board of directors. He accepted.

He learned Larry's story, as well as Ray's, Ron's, Samuel's, and many more.

Megan had their second child, and they named him after Larry. When asked why, he said they admired Larry's resilience and courage.

Blake and Megan sold their house. It was much more than they needed. They bought a smaller one they could better afford.

Blake continued to meet with Debbie. He admitted to her often that not meeting for all those years was one of the worst decisions of his life. He also decided to accept the invitation to join the group.

Debbie also explained the SERVE model to Blake in great detail. As you can imagine, for him to learn the practical ways that leaders serve helped his new team immensely.

Most importantly, through it all, Blake was getting his new heart. In quiet moments of reflection, Blake was able to acknowledge that he had been given an immeasurable gift. He was developing his father's heart. Now he and Megan turned their attention to passing this legacy on to their children.

Author's Note

Blake was one of the lucky ones. He was a leader who got it. He understood that one of life's greatest privileges is to serve others. He was also fortunate to have friends and family that would challenge him, support him, coach him, and love him.

As Blake discovered, a heart transplant is not easy. But it is a prize worth our full effort. When we learn about the HEART of leadership, we step into a world of possibilities. As the ancients believed, the heart is the source of all things. It may not be true biologically, but it is certainly true where leaders are concerned.

I don't know where you are on your journey. If, like Blake, you're one of the lucky ones, if you already "get it," let me encourage you to pass it on. Help an emerging leader cultivate the HEART of leadership.

If you're not there yet, welcome to the club. As I write this, I'm thankful for progress I've made over the years, and I maintain a painful awareness of how far I have to go. My gaps are obvious to me and those around me, but I'm not finished. My heart continues to change, and yours can, too. As long as we're willing to learn and grow, we can make a difference in the lives of others.

Enjoy the journey!

The Heart of Leadership
Self-Assessment

Rate each of the following statements using the following scale:
1 = Never; 2 = Rarely; 3 = Sometimes; 4 = Often; 5 = Always

Hunger for Wisdom

I see my personal development as one of my
highest priorities.   _____

My calendar reflects the high priority I place on the
pursuit of wisdom.   _____

I invest time on a regular basis with people who
help me grow.   _____

Self-evaluation and reflection play an active role in
my pursuit of wisdom.   _____

Expect the Best

When difficulties arise I remain optimistic.   _____

My "expect the best" outlook impacts all areas
of my life.   _____

I consistently demonstrate an "expect the best"
attitude.   _____

I am able to grasp reality and maintain my optimism.   _____

Accept Responsibility

I accept responsibility for my effort and outcomes.   _____

I willingly accept responsibility for the work of
those I lead.   _____

When outcomes are not good, I look to my role
in the situation first.   _____

When outcomes are good, I am quick to give praise.   _____

Respond with Courage

I am willing to make tough decisions.   _____

I maintain a high bias for action.   _____

People can count on me to do the right thing
even when it won't be popular.   _____

My first instinct when faced with a challenge or
opportunity is to act.   _____

Think Others First

I consider the needs and desires of others
before my own.   _____

I constantly look for ways to add value to others.   _____

During my daily activities, I often find myself
serving others.   _____

I am a serving leader.   _____

What's Next after the Assessment?

1. Look for critical gaps—work to close those first.

2. Look for ideas for personal application from Blake's mentors.

3. Create a plan for improvement. Share it with a friend, spouse, or mentor. Ask him or her to give you the gift of accountability.

4. Stay on the journey!

Acknowledgments

There are countless men and women to thank for their contributions to this project. When writing about a subject as complex as leadership character, with its roots running deep into our childhood, any list would be incomplete without acknowledging my parents, to whom I dedicated this book. Their unconditional love, high expectations, and unquestioned support were undoubtedly the primary drivers for who I am today.

But any attempt at a comprehensive list would have to include teachers, pastors, coaches, and friends who have also shaped my heart, my worldview, and my outlook on the future. To all of them who modeled leadership character for me, I will be forever grateful.

And then, there are my colleagues at Chick-fil-A. Over thirty-five years, I've had the privilege to work in a world-class leadership laboratory. I wish my writing skills and my vocabulary were up to the task to express what it's been like working with Truett Cathy for more than three decades. He and scores of other leaders within our staff have shown me the type of leadership character I've written about in this story. Thank you.

I also want to acknowledge the men and women who operate almost 2,000 Chick-fil-A restaurants. Their leadership is a constant inspiration to me and the 70,000-plus people they lead on a daily basis. Our restaurant Operators are our competitive advantage. Thanks for all you've taught me, and continue to teach me, about leadership character.

Finally, as I think about the book itself, I want to thank Ryan Bowman and Cathy Price. These two, more than anyone else, challenged me years ago to think about the 90 percent of leadership below the waterline. I've been thinking about it and I hope you approve of my conclusions. Thanks to Justin Whitfield who also challenged me to do this work. Thanks to my son, Justin, for his contributions. When some questioned the original premise of the book, it was Justin who convinced me to stay the course.

Thanks to my wife, Donna, for reading the manuscript—more than once. And thanks to the Berrett-Koehler staff and editors for believing in a guy who sells chicken for a living. I cannot mention their entire staff even though many of them have collaborated to make this book a reality, but I must thank Steve Piersanti for repeatedly challenging me to clarify and simplify my message. I tried.

I also want to acknowledge you—thank you for reading this book. My prayer is that it will serve you well.

About the Author

 Mark Miller is a business leader, best-selling author, and communicator.

Mark began his Chick-fil-A career working as an hourly team member in 1977. In 1978, Mark joined the corporate staff working in the warehouse and mailroom. Since that time, he has provided leadership for Corporate Communications, Field Operations, Quality and Customer Satisfaction, Training and Development, and today, he serves as the Vice President, Organizational Effectiveness. During his time with Chick-fil-A, annual sales have grown to almost five billion dollars. The company has more than 1,750 restaurants in thirty-nine states and the District of Columbia.

Mark began writing about a decade ago. He teamed up with Ken Blanchard, co-author of *The One Minute Manager,* to write *The Secret: What Great Leaders Know and Do.* Recently, he released *The Secret of Teams,* which outlines some of the key lessons learned from a twenty-year study on what makes some teams outperform the rest. His most recent book, *Great Leaders Grow: Becoming a Leader for Life,* was released in February 2012 and was co-authored with Ken Blanchard. Today, almost 600,000 copies of Mark's books are in print in twenty-eight languages.

In addition to his writing, Mark loves speaking to leaders. Over the years, he's traveled extensively around the world teaching for numerous international organizations. His theme is always the same: encouraging and equipping leaders. His topics include leadership, creativity, team building, and more.

Mark has an active lifestyle. As a photographer, he enjoys shooting in some of the world's hardest-to-reach places, including Mount Kilimanjaro, Antarctica, Everest Base Camp, and the jungles of Rwanda.

Mark is also active in social media. He'd love to connect with you via:

WEBSITE:	GreatLeadersServe.org
ON TWITTER:	@LeadersServe
ON FACEBOOK:	Great Leaders Serve
LINKEDIN:	Mark Miller

Also by Mark Miller

The Secret of Teams

What Great Teams Know and Do

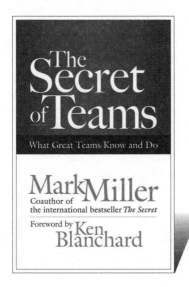

Teams are critical to the success of every organization. But what separates the teams that really deliver from the ones that simply spin their wheels? Mark Miller uses a compelling business fable to reveal critical insights that can dramatically transform any organization. Executive Debbie Brewster has been promoted and is now struggling with taking her new team to the next level. On her journey she learns from three very different teams—the Special Forces, NASCAR, and a local restaurant. Debbie and her team discover the three elements that all high-performing teams have in common, how to change entrenched ways of thinking and acting, what you have to do to optimize each of the three elements of a successful team, how to measure your progress, and more.

Hardcover, 144 pages, ISBN 978-1-60994-093-5
PDF ebook, ISBN 978-1-60994-109-3

BK® Berrett–Koehler Publishers, Inc.
San Francisco, www.bkconnection.com   **800.929.2929**

With Ken Blanchard

The Secret
What Great Leaders Know and Do, Second Edition

Join struggling young executive Debbie Brewster as she explores a profound yet seemingly contradictory concept: to lead is to serve. Along the way she learns why great leaders seem preoccupied with the future, what three arenas require continuous improvement, the two essential components to leadership success, how to knowingly strengthen—or unwittingly destroy—leadership credibility, and more.

Hardcover, 144 pages, ISBN 978-1-60509-268-3
PDF ebook, ISBN 978-1-60509-470-0

Great Leaders Grow
Becoming a Leader for Life

What is the secret to lasting as a leader? Debbie Brewster tells Blake, her mentor's son, whom she is now mentoring, "How well you and I serve will be determined by the decision to grow or not." As Debbie leads Blake through the four growth areas that every leader must focus on, you'll be inspired to make your own long-term plan for professional and personal growth.

Hardcover, 144 pages, ISBN 978-1-60994-303-5
PDF ebook, ISBN 978-1-60509-695-7

BK° Berrett–Koehler Publishers, Inc.
San Francisco, www.bkconnection.com   800.929.2929

Berrett–Koehler
Publishers

Berrett-Koehler is an independent publisher dedicated to an ambitious mission: *Connecting people and ideas to create a world that works for all.*

We believe that the solutions to the world's problems will come from all of us, working at all levels: in our organizations, in our society, and in our own lives. Our BK Business books help people make their organizations more humane, democratic, diverse, and effective (we don't think there's any contradiction there). Our BK Currents books offer pathways to creating a more just, equitable, and sustainable society. Our BK Life books help people create positive change in their lives and align their personal practices with their aspirations for a better world.

All of our books are designed to bring people seeking positive change together around the ideas that empower them to see and shape the world in a new way.

And we strive to practice what we preach. At the core of our approach is Stewardship, a deep sense of responsibility to administer the company for the benefit of all of our stakeholder groups including authors, customers, employees, investors, service providers, and the communities and environment around us. Everything we do is built around this and our other key values of quality, partnership, inclusion, and sustainability.

This is why we are both a B-Corporation and a California Benefit Corporation—a certification and a for-profit legal status that require us to adhere to the highest standards for corporate, social, and environmental performance.

We are grateful to our readers, authors, and other friends of the company who consider themselves to be part of the BK Community. We hope that you, too, will join us in our mission.

A BK Business Book

We hope you enjoy this BK Business book. BK Business books pioneer new leadership and management practices and socially responsible approaches to business. They are designed to provide you with groundbreaking and practical tools to transform your work and organizations while upholding the triple bottom line of people, planet, and profits. High-five!

To find out more, visit **www.bkconnection.com.**

Berrett–Koehler
Publishers

Connecting people and ideas
to create a world that works for all

Dear Reader,

Thank you for picking up this book and joining our worldwide community of Berrett-Koehler readers. We share ideas that bring positive change into people's lives, organizations, and society.

To welcome you, we'd like to offer you a free e-book. You can pick from among twelve of our bestselling books by entering the promotional code **BKP92E** here: http://www.bkconnection.com/welcome.

When you claim your free e-book, we'll also send you a copy of our e-newsletter, the *BK Communiqué*. Although you're free to unsubscribe, there are many benefits to sticking around. In every issue of our newsletter you'll find

- A free e-book
- Tips from famous authors
- Discounts on spotlight titles
- Hilarious insider publishing news
- A chance to win a prize for answering a riddle

Best of all, our readers tell us, "Your newsletter is the only one I actually read." So claim your gift today, and please stay in touch!

Sincerely,

Charlotte Ashlock
Steward of the BK Website

Questions? Comments? Contact me at bkcommunity@bkpub.com.

MIX
Paper from
responsible sources
FSC
www.fsc.org FSC® C011935

Certified

(B)

Corporation
bcorporation.net